Science Teaching Reconsidered

A · H · A · N · D · B · O · O · K

Committee on Undergraduate Science Education

National Academy Press
Washington, D.C. 1997

National Academy Press • 2101 Constitution Avenue, N.W., Washington, D.C. 20418

The project that is the subject of this report was approved by the Governing Board of the National Research Council, whose members are drawn from the councils of the National Academy of Sciences, the National Academy of Engineering, and the Institute of Medicine. The members of the committee responsible for the report were chosen for their special competences and with regard for appropriate balance.

This report has been reviewed by a group other than the authors according to procedures approved by a Report Review Committee consisting of members of the National Academy of Sciences, the National Academy of Engineering, and the Institute of Medicine.

The National Research Council was organized by the National Academy of Sciences in 1916 to associate the broad community of science and technology with the Academy's purposes of furthering knowledge and advising the federal government. Functioning in accordance with general policies determined by the Academy, the Council has become the principal operating agency of both the National Academy of Sciences and the National Academy of Engineering in providing services to the government, the public, and the scientific and engineering communities. The Council is administered jointly by both Academies and the Institute of Medicine. Dr. Bruce Alberts and Dr. William Wulf are chairman and interim vice chairman, respectively, of the National Research Council.

The Center for Science, Mathematics, and Engineering Education was established in 1995 to provide coordination of all the National Research Council's education activities and reform efforts for all students at all levels, specifically at the kindergarten through twelfth grade, undergraduate, school-to-work programs, and continuing education. The Center reports directly to the Governing Board of the National Research Council.

The views and conclusions contained in this document are those of the authors and should not be interpreted as representing the official policies, either expressed or implied, of the U.S. Government.

This study by the Committee on Undergraduate Science Education was conducted under National Academy of Sciences/National Research Council's Cooperative Agreement (No. OSR-935574) with the National Science Foundation. Any opinions, findings, conclusions, or recommendations expressed in this publication are those of the author(s) and do not necessarily reflect the view of the National Science Foundation.

Library of Congress Cataloging-in-Publication Data
Science teaching reconsidered : a handbook / [prepared by the]
    Committee on Undergraduate Science Education.
            p.   cm.
        Includes bibliographical references and index.
        ISBN 0-309-05498-2
        1. Science—Study and teaching (Higher)—Handbooks, manuals, etc.
    I. Committee on Undergraduate Science Education (U.S.)
    Q181.S3822 1997
    507'.1'173—dc21   97-4492
                                                                                          CIP

Additional copies of this report are available for sale from
National Academy Press
2101 Constitution Avenue, N.W.
Lock Box 285
Washington, D.C. 20055
800-624-6242 or 202-334-3313 (in the Washington metropolitan area)
This report is also available on-line at http://www.nap.edu.

COMMITTEE ON UNDERGRADUATE SCIENCE EDUCATION

C. BRADLEY MOORE, *Chair*, Professor of Chemistry, University of California, Berkeley

ISAAC D. ABELLA, Professor of Physics, University of Chicago, IL

NEAL B. ABRAHAM, Professor of Physics, Bryn Mawr College, Bryn Mawr, PA

GEORGE BOGGS, President, Palomar College, San Marcos, CA

DENICE D. DENTON, Associate Professor of Electrical and Computer Engineering, University of Wisconsin, Madison (After August, 1996: Dean, College of Engineering, University of Washington, Seattle)

MICHAEL P. DOYLE, Professor of Chemistry, Trinity University, San Antonio, TX

MARYE ANNE FOX, Vice President for Research, University of Texas, Austin

DOROTHY L. GABEL, Professor of Education, Indiana University, Bloomington

RAMESH GANGOLLI, Professor and Chair of Mathematics, University of Washington, Seattle

FREDERICK T. GRAYBEAL, Chief Geologist, ASARCO, Inc., New York, NY

NORMAN HACKERMAN, Chair, Scientific Advisory Board, The Robert A. Welch Foundation, Houston, TX

JOHN K. HAYNES, Professor of Biology, Morehouse College, Atlanta, GA

EILEEN DELGADO JOHANN, Professor of Chemistry, Miami-Dade Community College, FL

WILLIAM E. KIRWAN, President, University of Maryland, College Park

PAUL J. KUERBIS, Professor of Education, The Colorado College, Colorado Springs

SHARON LONG, Professor of Biology, Stanford University, CA

DOROTHY J. MERRITTS, Associate Professor of Geology, Franklin and Marshall College, Lancaster, PA

JOHN A. MOORE, Professor Emeritus of Biology, University of California, Riverside

PENNY P. MOORE, Teacher, Piedmont High School, Piedmont, CA

W. ANN REYNOLDS, Chancellor, City University of New York

JAMES W. SERUM, Manager, Advanced Sensor Products, Hewlett-Packard Corporation, Wilmington, DE

DAVID T. WILKINSON, Professor of Physics, Princeton University, Princeton, NJ

Contributing Author

BARBARA G. DAVIS, Assistant Vice Chancellor, Student Life & Educational Development, University of California, Berkeley

Staff

NANCY L. DEVINO, Study Director

JAY B. LABOV, Study Director (until July 1995)

PAMELA A. CAMPOS, Research Assistant (until May 1994)

MINNA A. MAHLAB, Research Assistant (until January 1997)

GAIL E. PRITCHARD, Research Assistant

CATHERINE Y. BELL, Project Assistant

STACEY N. PATMORE, Project Assistant (until October 1996)

Foreword

It is a privilege and a pleasure for me to introduce this handbook, three years in the making, designed to facilitate major changes in the way that science is taught to students in U.S. colleges and universities. A resource of this type would have been much appreciated in 1966, when I began as an Assistant Professor of Chemistry at Princeton University. I had a typical "good teachers are born, not made" attitude about teaching then. My present, very different view is that teaching is a skilled profession, which can only be learned through much study and experience. This view took 20 years to acquire, and it derives partly through my extensive contacts with elementary school teachers in San Francisco. Also influential was my later involvement with the National Research Council's National Science Education Standards, whose 25-page Chapter 3 Teaching Standards should greatly benefit teachers at any level (available at *www.nas.edu*). Research has taught us a great deal about effective teaching and learning in recent years, and scientists should be no more willing to fly blind in their teaching than they are in scientific research, where no new investigation is begun without an extensive examination of what is already known.

What we do today in our classrooms is much more important than most faculty imagine. Those of us who teach undergraduate science must greatly expand our view of our mission. Our role cannot simply be to teach the basic facts and concepts of our discipline, so as to prepare students for the next science course that they may decide to take on their route to medical or graduate school. Our colleges and universities will graduate approximately two million students next year, only about 15% of whom will receive bachelor's degrees in science or engineering. All the rest will become the citizens who determine—by their understanding and appreciation for the nature and values of science—both the vitality of our nation and the future of our scientific enterprise. It would be fine if all Americans knew about plate tectonics, or the way that cells divide. But it is much more important that they understand what science is (and what it is not) and how its central values—honesty, generosity, and respect for the ideas of others—have made possible the rationalization of human experience that underlies all human progress.

These understandings are important for all Americans, but they are especially crucial for those students in our introductory science classes who will go on to become the next generation of teachers. It is unreasonable to expect our elementary, middle, and high school teachers to be effective in teaching science as an inquiry-based process, if they have never experienced inquiry themselves. Instead, we can all be expected to teach as we ourselves were taught, which explains why I only lectured at the students as a Princeton professor.

The cycle must end. This handbook is a valuable introductory tool that presents research-based thinking and the practice of teaching by scientists who are committed educators. But *Science Teaching Reconsidered* needs to be embedded in a much larger process that will change people, institutions and systems. We hope that this handbook will be incorporated into an action plan for reform of undergraduate education, to which the Academy will continue to contribute.

Bruce Alberts
President, National Academy of Sciences

Preface

Science Teaching Reconsidered is a practical handbook designed for college teachers who want to explore new ways to enhance student learning. The handbook draws on the knowledge of teachers and scientists with extensive experiences in the natural sciences and a keen interest in effective science teaching. This handbook is designed especially for new faculty members and graduate teaching assistants, but is intended to be useful to anyone interested in teaching undergraduate science, whether it be in a research university, liberal arts college, or community college.

How often do all of us ask ourselves: What do I want students to learn from this course? What are they actually learning? What mix of factual information and conceptual understanding best serves my students' needs? How do I decide which teaching methods work best for my students? How do I measure student learning? This handbook is designed to help you find answers to such questions.

Effective science instruction is an art involving creativity, imagination, and innovation, along with planning, practice, decision making, and evaluation. Teaching is a scholarly activity, benefiting from research, collective experience, and critical thinking throughout. Yet with all the demands on our time we seldom have an opportunity to think through the entire process. This handbook should help you to review some basic principles underlying current issues in science education, to think about how you might assess your own teaching, and to design ways to increase its effectiveness.

Science Teaching Reconsidered does not focus on scientific course content. Rather, it provides information about successful teaching practices in a variety of science courses. It offers you an overview of current research in undergraduate science education and some practical guidelines for experimenting with and changing the ways you teach. While we believe that the chapters are closely related, we have tried to design each chapter to stand alone so that they may be read in any order. The references and related on-line database listings have been chosen to provide more details about the teaching and learning processes discussed; the list is by no means comprehensive.

Some readers may want more scholarly depth, but please keep in mind that this handbook is a practical guide to help busy teachers learn about and try new ways to enhance student learning. Continued engagement with these issues may lead you to regular perusal of disciplinary or interdisciplinary journals and/or to participation in local, professional, or electronic discussion groups. Sources listed in the appendices are a good starting point for further study.

The committee expresses its deep gratitude to the hundreds of teachers, from dozens of colleges and universities, who were crucial to the assessment and substantial revisions of two early versions of this handbook. Not only was much of your advice heeded, your obvious dedication to good teaching was inspiring.

Table of Contents

Appendices

Science Teaching Reconsidered

A · H · A · N · D · B · O · O · K

1

How Teachers Teach: General Principles

- How to develop a teaching style that is best suited to your course goals and students' needs.
- How to plan a course syllabus that will maximize your students' learning.
- What research tells us about effective teaching.

Have you ever observed your students struggling with a particular concept, then revised your presentation of that material the next semester? Have you ever concluded that the only way to reach some students is with a specific strategy, such as using demonstrations or requiring written assignments? Has someone ever told you about a favorite teaching strategy that sounded exciting, but when you tried it in your own class, it did not work for you and your students? If you answered yes to any of these questions, you have been learning about teaching through your experiences with students. In other words, you have been experimenting with ways of teaching, using observations of your students and their learning to draw inferences, make generalizations, and develop your own model of teaching and learning. Teaching is much more difficult than most faculty are willing to acknowledge:

> "The assumption that knowledge of a subject implies the ability to teach in that field permeates American higher education, and one result is that our colleagues generally believe that the problems associated with teaching should disappear as the competent scholar eases past the initial nervousness" (Fraher, 1984).

For those interested in going beyond their own experiences, the science education literature provides ideas and information about teaching and learning. Appendices A and B provide a list of organizations that can be contacted for information and journals which can serve as an introduction to this body of scholarship. The successful strategies used by science faculty in many different disciplines are a good source of ideas to adapt for your own classes. Meetings of professional societies often include workshops on teaching in a given discipline. In addition, experts in science education research publish their work in peer-reviewed journals; those of you seeking evidence that a particular method is effective may find these articles helpful. There are also books on the art of teaching in a specific discipline (Arons, 1990; Herron, 1996). The objective of Chapters 1 and 2 is to acquaint you with the general principles and results of science education research and to provide examples of how these results have been translated into classroom practice so that you can improve your teaching as efficiently as possible.

TEACHING AND LEARNING

Teaching and learning should be inseparable, in that learning is a criterion and product of effective teaching. In essence, learning is the goal of teaching. Someone has not taught unless someone else has learned. After a few years of teaching, many faculty realize that students learn too little of what they teach. Science teaching requires attention to both the content of the course and the process of moving students from their initial state of knowledge and understanding to the desired level. In fact, teaching is part of a whole that comprises the teacher, the learner, the disciplinary content, the teaching/learning process, and the evaluation of both the teacher and the learner.

Undergraduate students value good teaching, and many of those who switch from a science major to another field cite poor teaching as an important factor in their decision (Seymour and Hewitt, 1994). When the data from students who persist in a science major was combined with data from students who switched out of a science major, poor teaching by science faculty was the students' most frequently cited concern. Although students are turned off by poor teaching, they also have identified characteristics of good teaching:

- a teacher's enthusiasm and passion for the subject,
- rapport between a teacher and a student or group of students during discussions in and out of class,
- intellectual challenges from a teacher,
- clarity and organization in presenting analytical and conceptual understanding of ideas, and
- a teacher's scholarship.

Teaching Styles

Research indicates that teachers teach in a manner consistent with their own way of learning (Shulman, 1990; Tobin et al., 1994). However, it is not necessarily true that student learning can be understood from the teachers' own learning history. What is your style of learning? Do you learn most easily if material is presented to you in a formal and structured manner, or do you learn most easily if you are forced to discover basic principles from a series of exercises and examples? Do you believe that your students will learn best if you use a teaching style that helped you learn as a student? Studies of teaching and learning have led to classification of teaching styles into three general categories: discipline-centered, instructor-centered, and student-centered (Dressel and Marcus, 1982; Woods, 1995).

In *discipline-centered teaching*, the course has a fixed structure. The needs, concerns, and requirements of teacher and student are not considered because the course is driven by and depends mainly on the disciplinary content that must be presented. The teacher transmits information, but the content is dictated by some separate authority such as a department syllabus committee or textbook author.

The teacher acts as a model of the educated person in *instructor-centered teaching.* He or she is regarded as the authoritative expert, the main source of knowledge, and the focal point of all activity. The student is the passive recipient of the information already acquired by the teacher. The teacher selects from the discipline the information to be taught, studied, and learned.

Student-centered teaching focuses on the student and, in particular, on the cognitive development of the student. The teacher's goal is to help students grasp the development of knowledge as a process rather than a product. The focus of classroom activities and assignments is on the student-centered process of inquiry itself, not on the products of inquiry. Students create their own conceptual or cognitive models. Content, teaching style, and methods are adapted to aid the cognitive and intellectual growth of students. Student-centered teaching combines an understanding of the way that humans process information with other factors that affect learning such as attitudes, values, beliefs, and motivation.

Although there are many ways to teach effectively, all require that the teacher have knowledge of three things: 1) the material being taught; 2) the best instructional strategies to teach the material (see Chapter 2); and 3) how students learn (discussed more fully in Chapter 3). New faculty members typically know far more about the content of their discipline than they do about instructional strategies, and therefore tend to use teaching styles similar to those used by their own teachers (Shulman, 1990). In most cases, they use elements of all three general teaching styles. As the teacher gains experience, his or her teaching style is likely to change.

What is the most effective way to teach students? The answer depends on what students are expected to learn. Students taught by lectures, instructor-centered presentations, and student-centered methods achieve similar results on tests that measure factual knowledge. However, student-centered discussions lead to better retention, better transfer of knowledge to other situations, better motivation for further learning, and better problem-solving ability (McKeachie, 1994). Active participation by students helps them construct a better framework from which to generalize their knowledge.

Developing a Teaching Style

The first step in preparing to teach a particular course is to decide on a particular style of teaching that is compatible with and appropriate for your students and the goals of your course. It is likely that you will use a combination of the three teaching styles, depending on the circumstances of your course. While developing their own teaching style, science teachers must answer a fundamental question: Is the primary goal of my course for each student to gain specific information, or for each student to master how to organize and apply new information independently to new situations? The primary goal may not be the same for each student in a course, especially when the students come from diverse backgrounds (see Chapter 8). In courses that are the foundation for more advanced learning in a subject area, how should the content be organized and presented? Because science curricula tend to be vertically structured, students' content knowledge is critical for advancement in a field and for understanding the next level of information. In science courses for nonscience majors, how should the content be organized and presented? In any given course, we should ask what should be the balance between specific information, application of that information, and conceptual understanding of basic principles? If the course is truly to be a course for lawyers, citizens, teachers, and other nonscientists, it should provide some of the essence of what science is and the nature of the scientific enterprise.

Most science courses, particularly introductory courses, emphasize discipline-centered teaching. Generations of students have been exposed to science as a subject in which the correct formulas and answers must be memorized, and the material is divided into many different and seemingly unrelated pieces. Problems with this approach have been exacerbated by the explosion of scientific information. Faculty members, wishing to cover the latest results and ideas but reluctant to discard classical material, rush to cover more and more information in the same amount of time.

Those who have studied the learning of science have concluded that students learn best if they are engaged in active learning, if they are forced to deal with observations and concepts before terms and facts, and if they have the sense that they are part of a community of learners in a classroom environment that is very supportive of their learning (Fraser, 1986; Chickering and Gamson, 1987; McDermott et al., 1987; Fraser and Tobin, 1989; McDermott, 1991; McDermott et al., 1994; McKeachie, 1994; Tobin et al., 1994). Instructor-centered and student-centered teaching are more effective than is discipline-centered teaching for students to learn in this way. When the focus is on meaning rather than solely on facts, students develop their conceptual abilities. They assimilate information by incorporating new concepts or by using information to differentiate among already existing concepts. This is not necessarily at the expense of their development of algorithmic abilities, because conceptual understanding gives a context for the application of problem-solving methods. A student-centered style is more likely to motivate students by engaging their interest. Several factors can influence your choice of teaching style:

- student needs (future course and career requirements, preparation for participatory citizenship, and preparation for careers in science, engineering, technology, or education),
- student background (preconceptions and misconceptions; see Chapter 4),
- familiarity with various teaching methods,
- course enrollment (size, students with special needs, the logistics of managing small group activities),
- student learning styles,
- teaching load (number of contact hours, office hours, time for preparation and grading),
- other responsibilities (research, committee work, administrative duties),
- support structures (equipment cost, teaching and demonstration assistants),

Collaborative Syllabus Design

Often, multiple sections of an introductory course are taught by different faculty members. Some faculty members find it useful to meet with their colleagues to design a syllabus that optimizes the order and structure in which to present the course material. For example, if you are teaching atomic theory, is it best to start with basic terms and then to build up to a model, or to start with a model and disassemble it piece by piece? The first step in collaborative syllabus design is to meet with fellow faculty members who teach the same course to identify basic concepts. Then, separately, each teacher does an analysis of the critical variables related to each concept. Finally, the colleagues reassemble to compare their lists, identify similarities and differences, and discuss the implications of their lists for instruction.

- facilities (laboratory equipment and computers, classroom and laboratory space, and demonstration equipment), and
- parallel sections that require some uniformity of coverage and examination.

In some circumstances, teachers must use methods that emphasize the imparting and acquiring of basic information and skills. Time constraints, class size, or course goals may lead to an emphasis on factual knowledge at the expense of developing a conceptual framework. Students are usually encouraged to accept facts from some authority (e.g., the instructor or the text) without questioning. If all their learning is rote learning, however, students seldom associate the new facts with concepts or models already part of their pictures of the world (A Private Universe, 1989). Chapter Two presents some methods teachers can use to promote active learning in a lecture setting.

What can be done about the many options, goals, and competing pressures? Current practice is not to prescribe one teaching style as best for a given course or type of student. Various methods for engaging students are applied successfully in a wide range of institutional settings. Some of these methods are discussed in more detail in the next chapter, and references to others are given to help you make an informed choice of style.

HOW SHOULD YOU PLAN A COURSE SYLLABUS?

How teachers teach is influenced to a great degree by what they teach and by how their courses are organized. The usual focus in organizing a course is the content. A syllabus typically includes the organization of topics into an outline of the course of study, readings, exercises, examinations, and grading scheme. These features are important, but it is equally important to identify the goals of the course (content, student responsibilities, and desired outcomes) and to work both forward (from the starting point of the

---

Connecting Science to the Social Sciences

Daniel D. Perlmutter of the University of Pennsylvania has developed a course called "Perspectives on Energy and the Environment." The goal of this course, which was taught for the first time in the 1994-1995 school year, is to provide nonscience majors with a quantitative understanding of science and technology. The course fulfills the University's Physical Science requirement and is open to students who are not science, math, or engineering majors. It emphasizes applications to current energy and environmental issues and focuses on techniques and approaches to problem solving. Men and women who do not have professional interests in science and engineering still need to become informed in these areas in order to function effectively in a complex world. This course approaches the matter of technical literacy from the point of view of a curious and motivated newspaper reader, for whom reports are available on a daily basis that provide a mix of engineering and public policy issues.

The material draws heavily upon information from recent news reports on subjects having to do with energy or environmental matters. In each case the technical and policy issues are summarized and where appropriate brief calculations check the assertions of the reporter or experts cited in the article. Having seen such examples, the student will be sensitized to the relevant scientific questions that bear on an issue, and may recognize how technical limitations on what is or is not possible can form bases for preliminary judgments on the merits of a controversy. Most important of all, when information is lacking for a full assessment to be made, the student will have a framework for asking appropriate questions that can serve to elicit the necessary additional details.

students) and backward (from the desired outcome of student understanding) to develop your syllabus. Student behaviors such as developing abilities to work in groups might also be included.

Research on how students learn science offers three fundamental guidelines for course design (Novak and Gowin, 1984):

- Become aware of the students' prior knowledge and take it into account (see also Chapters 3 and 4).
- Identify the major and minor concepts and the connections between different concepts.
- Relate new information to a context the student understands. Along with repetition and application, these relationships are extremely important for student retention of the material.

To achieve these goals, a syllabus might include the following (Novak, 1977; Davis, 1993):

- overview of the course's purpose, including a rationale for why students should learn the material,
- the learning goals or objectives (what students should know or be able to do after completing the course),
- the conceptual structure used to organize the course,
- the important topics covered by the course,
- sequencing of topics so that major concepts are introduced early and can be reinforced through application to new situations,
- identification of the methods and accuracy of inquiry used to develop concepts and to identify the major information of the field,
- important knowledge, skills, or experience students need to succeed in the course, and
- evaluation and feedback strategies.

A Multidisciplinary Lab at Princeton University

Professors: Rosemary Grant, Maitland Jones, Shirley Tilghman, and David Wilkinson
Enrollment: 30-50 students
"Origins and Beginnings" is a year-long course intended for students who may take no other science courses in college. Some fundamental ideas from physics, chemistry, molecular biology, and evolutionary biology are developed around questions associated with origins of life and origins of the human condition. The course is designed to engage students in the scientific process. During the first half of the term, students learn basic concepts and practice a few prescribed laboratory techniques. In the second half of the term, groups of two or three students do research projects chosen from a list of topics. Equipment and materials are supplied, but the students plan and execute the experiment and analyze the results, all with the guidance of an instructor. Instructors emphasize that understanding the results is more important than whether the results are "correct."

For example, the physics/chemistry term introduces students to optical and infrared spectroscopy, computer modeling of molecular structure, and some wet lab techniques used in organic chemistry. Lectures, readings, and class discussion show how these techniques are used to study the molecular and environmental bases of life. Topics for student research projects include: Spectra of Light Reflected from Planets, the Solar Spectrum, Green House Gases, Pasteur's Experiment, Polycyclic Hydrocarbons, Computer-Generated Models, Constituents of Vegetables, and Bard's Experiment (making life's molecules in a bottle). Open-ended problems are chosen so that students have an opportunity to be creative and to try their own ideas.

HOW CAN I BROADEN THE CONTENT IN MY COURSE?

Science should be considered as intrinsically multi-disciplinary. Student learning is enhanced when we are able to help students see the relationships among the sciences, and between science and mathematics, the humanities, social sciences, and the arts. Organizing courses around themes, issues, or projects not only can broaden student thinking and problem-solving abilities, but also can enrich the students' view of science as a multi-faceted enterprise.

SHOULD YOU TEACH DIFFERENTLY TO FUTURE PRECOLLEGE TEACHERS?

Many lament the quality of science education for children in elementary, middle, and high schools, yet all precollege teachers were once undergraduates, and almost all teachers took introductory science classes to learn about the science they now must teach. Some even have argued that one of the main causes of the crisis in science education is the failure of colleges and universities to do an adequate job of preparing future science teachers (McDermott, 1990). The heart of the matter is this: improving undergraduate science education has a direct, positive effect on precollege education. An undergraduate science teacher who models real scientific skills of investigation and critical thinking, and applies those skills to new situations, can make an enormous contribution to the education of those students who will not only use the model, but eventually will teach it.

Should we teach present or future teachers differently from other students in our science classes? Most teachers of undergraduates have students in their classes who will need to share scientific understanding and skills with others, perhaps as a trial lawyer or a track coach, or as a member of a citizen's action group. Some of your students will likely become science teachers at the elementary level and have the opportunity to introduce curious children to important scientific concepts. Others may become secondary science teachers with responsibility for teaching advanced courses for college-bound students. Those who have studied science teaching are divided over how best to teach future science teachers. Some argue that future teachers need distinctly different instruction that is more hands-on, active, and problem oriented than what a future scientist might need. Others argue that future teachers need the same type of instruction as scientists; in other words, the future teacher should be treated like a future scientist while learning. Faculty members who are concerned about the preparation of K-12 teachers may want to meet with their colleagues in departments of education to discuss possible collaborative efforts.

This issue is unlikely to be resolved in the near future. Nevertheless, a vision of effective science teaching at the K-12 level has been analyzed and presented in a number of recent reform documents. These include Science for All Americans (American Association for the Advancement of Science, 1990b), The Content Core (National Science Teachers Association, 1992), Benchmarks for Science Literacy (American Association for the Advancement of Science, 1993), and The National Science Education Standards (National Research Council, 1996). These reports can be helpful to undergraduate science teachers who are concerned about how best to assist future K-12 teachers to become as effective as possible. One overarching theme in all of these reform efforts is the recognition of a need to teach in a manner that engages students in using complex reasoning in authentic contexts.

2

How Teachers Teach: Specific Methods

- Methods for making your class sessions more effective
- Ways to encourage student participation in your classes
- Advantages of collaborative learning
- Examples of effective laboratory practices

This chapter discusses several methods of teaching science within the traditional formats: lectures, discussion sessions, and laboratories. How can you help your students learn science better and more efficiently in each format? Although there is no universal best way to teach, experience shows that some general principles apply (American Association for the Advancement of Science, 1990a; McDermott et al., 1994; Mazur, 1996):

- Teach scientific ways of thinking.
- Actively involve students in their own learning.
- Help students to develop a conceptual framework as well as to develop problem-solving skills.
- Promote student discussion and group activities.
- Help students experience science in varied, interesting, and enjoyable ways.
- Assess student understanding at frequent intervals throughout the learning process.

LECTURES

Evidence from a number of disciplines suggests that oral presentations to large groups of passive students contribute very little to real learning. In physics, standard lectures do not help most students develop conceptual understanding of fundamental processes in electricity and in mechanics (Arons, 1983; McDermott and Shaffer, 1992; McDermott et al., 1994). Similarly, student grades in a large general chemistry lecture course do not correlate with the lecturing skills and experience of the instructor (Birk and Foster, 1993).

9

Enhancing Learning in Large Classes

Despite the limitations of traditional lectures, many institutions are forced to offer high-enrollment introductory science courses. Many professors who teach these courses feel that lecturing is their only option, and can only dream of what they could accomplish in smaller classes. However, there is a small but growing group of science faculty members who have developed ways to engage students in the process of thinking, questioning, and problem solving despite the large class size. Strategies in use in introductory courses in biology and geology are described in the sidebars.

Although many of the methods described in these sidebars are consistent with what experts know about how students learn (see Chapter 3), they may not be welcomed by all of the students in a class. There are several ways to help students make the transition from passive listeners to active participants in their own learning (Orzechowksi, 1995):

- Start off slowly; students may not have much experience in active learning.
- Introduce change at the beginning of a course, rather than midway through.
- Avoid giving students the impression that you are "experimenting" with them.

Biochemistry, Genetics, and Molecular Biology at Stanford University

Professor: Sharon Long
Enrollment: 400 students

One important tool I use to engage students is to create opportunities for thought and for active pursuit of an unknown during the class session. If I give a lecture for which I provide notes—a common practice—I always leave blanks in critical parts of the notes. On the board or transparency, I indicate the unknown. I pause while I talk about it, drawing the students' attention to the hole in the notes. If possible, I ask for suggested answers or for a vote among the possibilities. By arranging the pause in your lecture you can give the students the chance to puzzle out the question themselves and to preview their ability to work on the questions independently. And only by attending class can a student gain all the information—an important draw to encourage class attendance.

In teaching formal genetics, I draw out a genetic cross first in general form (in this example, a Drosophila eye color inheritance test):

$$w^+y \; x \; w\,w$$

Then I put into the lecture notes a completely blank Punnett square to show the structure of the approach—but not to provide the answer.

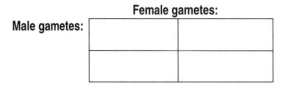

The students encounter this as an unknown, because I address the contents of each line, and each box, as a question. (Everybody, consult with your neighbor for a minute—now second row, anybody tell me, what should be in these two blanks at the top? What would be the genotype and phenotype for the bottom right box?)

Physical Geology at Arizona State University

Professor: Ramon Arrowsmith
Enrollment: 220 students

I show examples of geology from my own experiences, and occasionally include a few funny slides or video or audio clips to lighten things up. I use a multimedia presentation system composed of a vertical camera above an illuminated table on which I write or place rocks, examples from the book, or anything else I want the students to see. The video signal is projected on a screen in the classroom. This form of presentation has worked well and definitely has improved students' access to the material by making things more visible. Along with the presentation system, I use a laser disc containing movies and photographs from a textbook publisher. I can easily switch from multimedia to laser disc output and thus weave visual examples into my lecture. Occasionally, I show the students computer files or video from a VHS player. The students react well to this multimedia approach, but to involve the students I have them do a short exercise in groups, then we talk about it.

For these, I walk up the side of the auditorium and designate even and odd rows. Then I say that the even people should turn around and face the odd people and do the exercise together. This generates groups of 2-6 people. They all put their names onto the single sheet they are to turn in. Then the students work together on a question for 3-4 minutes. I walk around the room, answering their questions.

When time is up, the TA stands at the overhead projector, and I walk through the crowd (I have a lapel mike so they can hear me), collecting their answers for each question. Then we talk about solutions. Usually the time runs out, and the students turn their papers. Of course, they get credit for their participation, and that provides some motivation, but I am sure students understand the concepts better than if they were presented only in my lecture.

This process engages the students. Of course the hub-bub grows as the students move from the assigned topic to other conversations, but they come back fairly quickly. It is a bit unnerving because there is the potential for loss of control in the class, but the students seem to either like it or are indifferent, but certainly aren't quite as passive as they are while being lectured at.

- Don't give up lectures completely.
- Anticipate students' anxiety, and be prepared to provide support and encouragement as they adapt to your expectations.
- Discuss your approach with colleagues, especially if you are teaching a well-established course in a pre-professional curriculum.

Hints for More Effective Lecturing

When lecturing is the chosen or necessary teaching method, one way to keep students engaged is to pause periodically to assess student understanding or to initiate short student discussions (see sidebars). Calling on individual students to answer questions or offer comments can also hold student attention; however, some students prefer a feedback method with more anonymity. If they have an opportunity to discuss a question in small groups, the group can offer an answer, which removes any one student from the spotlight. Another option is to have students write their answer on an index card, and pass the card to the end of the row; the student seated there can select one answer to present, without disclosing whose it is.

The literature on teaching and learning contains other examples of techniques to maintain students' attention in a lecture setting (Eble, 1988; Davis, 1993; Lowman, 1995; McKeachie, 1994):

- Avoid direct repetition of material in a textbook so that it remains a useful alternative resource.

- Use paradoxes, puzzles, and apparent contradictions to engage students.
- Make connections to current events and everyday phenomena.
- Begin each class with something familiar and important to students.
- End each class by summarizing the main points you have made.
- Adopt a reasonable and adjustable pace that balances content coverage and student understanding.
- Consider using slides, videos, films, CD-ROMs, and computer simulations to enhance presentations, but remember that:
  → Students cannot take notes in darkened rooms.
  → The text needs to be large enough to read from the back of the room.
  → Students need time to summarize their observations and to draw and note conclusions.
- Pay attention to delivery:
  → Maintain eye contact with students in all parts of the room.
  → Step out from behind the lecture bench when feasible.
  → Move around, but not so much that it is distracting.
  → Talk to the students, not the blackboard.
  → If using the board, avoid blocking it with AV projectors or screens.
  → Shift the mood and intensity.
  → Vary presentation techniques.

At the beginning of a course, discuss with your students several strategies for effectively engaging in and learning from your classes. Some may just listen, others will take notes, and still others may try to transcribe your words. Some students may want to tape the class session. If you want to encourage a particular form of student participation, make clear your expectations, the reasons for them, and how students' learning will benefit.

Asking Questions

Whether in lecture, discussion sections, laboratories, or individual encounters, questioning is an important part of guiding students' learning. When students ask questions, they are often seeking to shortcut the learning process by getting the right answer from an authority figure. However, it is the processes of arriving at an answer and assessing the validity of an answer that are usually more important, particularly if the student can apply these processes to the next question. Both of these processes are obscured if the teacher simply gives the requested answer. Often, the Socratic method—meeting a student's question with another (perhaps leading) question—forces students (while often frustrating them) to offer possible answers, supporting reasons, and assessments. In fact, posing questions can be an effective teaching technique. Here are some tips for the effective use of questions:

- Wait long enough to indicate that you expect students to think before answering. Some students know that if they are silent the professor will give the answer (Rowe, 1974).
- Solicit the answer from a volunteer or a selected student.
- Determine the student's confidence level as you listen to the answer.
- Solicit alternative answers or elaboration to provide material for comparison, contrast, and assessment.
- Solicit additional responses from the same students with a leading question or follow-up observation.

- Direct the ensuing discussion to the comparison, evaluation, and extension of the offered answers rather than simple validation or refutation of right and wrong answers.
- Pose a second or follow-up question to continue the exploration.

Biochemistry, Genetics, and Molecular Biology at Stanford University

Professor: Sharon Long
Enrollment: 400 students

Even a small-scale demonstration can work in a large class if it uses an everyday object that students recognize, and especially if it is something the students can find and use on their own. My favorite example is to use a telephone cord to demonstrate supercoiling of DNA. The phone cord has its own intrinsic helicity, as does DNA, though usually phone cords are left handed whereas DNA is most often discussed in its right handed B form.

Who doesn't have the experience of having the coiled headset cord of a telephone show supercoils (twists around itself)? This presents the students with the chance to play at home, where they can convince themselves that the direction (handedness) of the supercoils depends on the direction of the original helix, and on whether the cord was underwound or overwound before the headset was replaced (constraining the ends). Students learn both an important principle for understanding nucleic acids and a handy practical tip that lets them predict the easiest way to get the kinks out of the phone cord! They get the chance to test their understanding by making predictions and doing trials—exactly what one hopes for in active scientific learning.

A professor's questions should build confidence rather than induce fear. One technique is to encourage the student to propose several different answers to the question. The student can then be encouraged to step outside the answers and begin to develop the skills necessary to assess the answers. Some questions seek facts and simply measure student recall; others demand higher reasoning skills such as elaborating on or explaining a concept, comparing and contrasting several possibilities, speculating about an outcome, and speculating about cause and effect. The type of question asked and the response given to students' initial answers are crucial to the types of reasoning processes the students are encouraged to use. Several aspects of questions—how to formulate them, what reasoning or knowledge is tested or encouraged, how to deal with answers—are similar for dialogue and for testing. Chapters 5 and 6 contain more information on questions as part of assessment, testing, and grading.

Demonstrations

Demonstrations can be very effective for illustrating concepts in class, but can result in passive learning without careful attention to engaging students. They can provoke students to think for themselves and are especially helpful if the demonstration has a surprise, challenges an assumption, or illustrates an otherwise abstract concept or mechanism. Demonstrations that use everyday objects are especially effective and require little preparation on the part of faculty (see sidebar). Students' interest is peaked if they are asked to make predictions and vote on the most probable outcome. There are numerous resources available to help faculty design and conduct demonstrations. Many science education periodicals contain one or more demonstrations in each issue. The "Tested Demonstrations" column in the *Journal of Chemical Education* and the "Favorite Demonstration" column in the *Journal of College Science Teaching* are but two of the many examples. The American Chemical Society and the University of Wisconsin Press have published excellent books on chemical demonstrations (Shakhashiri, 1983, 1985, 1989, 1992; Summerlin and Ealy, 1985; Summerlin et al., 1987). Similar volumes of physics demonstrations have been published by the American Association of Physics Teachers (Freier and Anderson, 1981; Berry, 1987).

You should consider a number of issues when planning a demonstration (O'Brien, 1990):

- What concepts do you want the demonstration to illustrate?
- Which of the many demonstrations on the selected topic will generate the greatest enhancement in student learning?

- • Where in the class would it be most effective?
- • What prior knowledge should be reviewed before the demonstration?
- • What design would be most effective, given the materials at hand and the target audience?
- • Which steps in the demonstration procedure should be carried out ahead of time?
- • What questions will be appropriate to motivate and direct student observation and thought processes before, during, and after the demonstration?
- • What follow-up questions can be used to test and stretch students' understanding of the new concept?

If the classroom or lecture hall is large, consider whether students in the back will be able to see your demonstration. Look into videotaping the demonstration and projecting the image on a larger screen so that all of your students can see.

DISCUSSIONS

Small group discussion sections often are used in large-enrollment courses to complement the lectures. In courses with small enrollments, they can substitute for the lecture, or both lecture and discussion formats can be used in the same class period. The main distinction between lecture and discussion is the level of student participation that is expected, and a whole continuum exists. Discussions can be instructor-centered (students answer the instructor's questions) or student-centered (students address one another, and the instructor mainly guides the discussion toward important points). In any case, discussion sessions are more productive when students are expected to prepare in advance.

Why Discussion?

Focused discussion is an effective way for many students to develop their conceptual frameworks and to learn problem-solving skills as they try out their own ideas on other students and the instructor. The give and take of technical discussion also sharpens critical and quantitative thinking skills. Classes in which students must participate in discussion force them to go beyond merely plugging numbers into formulas or memorizing terms. They must learn to explain in their own words what they are thinking and doing. Students are more motivated to prepare for a class in which they are expected to participate actively.

However, student-centered discussions are less predictable than instructor-centered presentations, they are more time consuming, and they can require more skill from the teacher. To lead an effective discussion, the teacher must be a good facilitator, by ensuring that key points are covered and monitoring the group dynamics. Guidance is needed to keep the discussion from becoming disorganized or irrelevant. Some students do not like or may not function effectively in a class where much of the time is devoted to student discussion. Some may take the point of view that they have paid to hear the expert (the teacher). For them, and for all students, it is useful to review the benefits of discussion-based formats in contrast with lectures whose purpose is to transmit information.

Sensitivity to personality, cultural, linguistic, and gender differences that may affect students' participation in discussions is also important, especially if participation is graded. When students do not spontaneously engage in a discussion, they may be unprepared or they may be reluctant to speak or to be assertive. Some may be more comfortable making comparisons than absolute statements, and others may be more comfortable with narrative descriptions than with quantitative analysis. You might try various strategies to engage your students in meaningful discussion by posing questions that measure different levels of understanding (knowledge, application, analysis, and comprehension; see Chapter 6).

Planning and Guiding Discussions

Probably the best overall advice is to be bold but flexible and willing to adjust your strategies to fit the character of your class. If you want to experiment with using discussions in your class, here are some things to consider:

- Decide on the goals of your class discussion. What is it that you want the students to get from each class session? Concepts? Problem-solving skills? Decision-making skills? The ability to make connections to other disciplines or to technology? Broader perspective? Keep in mind that the goals may change as you progress through the material during the quarter or semester.
- Explain to the students how discussions will be structured. Will the discussion involve the whole class or will students work in smaller groups? Make clear what you expect them to do before coming to each class session: read the chapter, think about the questions at the end of the chapter, seriously try to do the first five problems, etc. Let students see you take attendance. Students who do not come to class may not be studying.
- If you want students to discuss questions and concepts in small groups, explain to students how the groups will form.
- Do not allow a few students to dominate the discussion. Some students will naturally respond more quickly, but they must be encouraged to let others have a chance. Be sure that all students participate at an acceptable level. In extreme cases you may have to speak outside of class to an aggressive or an excessively reticent student.
- Look for opportunities for you or your students to bring to class mini-demonstrations illustrating important points of the day's topic. This is a very effective way to stimulate discussion.
- Be willing to adjust to the needs of your students and to take advantage of your own strengths as a teacher. Watch for signs that the students need more or less guidance. Are the main points coming out and getting resolved? Do you need to do more summarizing or moderating?

COLLABORATIVE LEARNING

Collaborative learning "is an umbrella term for a variety of educational approaches involving joint intellectual effort by students, or students and teachers together" (Goodsell et al., 1992). Cooperative learning, a form of collaborative learning, is an instructional technique in which students work in groups to achieve a common goal, to which they each contribute in individually accountable ways (Stover et al., 1993). The interaction itself can take different forms:

- out-of-class study groups
- in-class discussion groups
- project groups (in and/or out of class)
- groups in which roles (leader, timekeeper, technician, spokesperson, and so forth) are assigned and rotated

Although cooperative learning has been used effectively in elementary, middle, and high schools for a number of years, as discussed by Johnson and Johnson (1989) and Slavin (1989), few studies have been done to demonstrate its effectiveness in the college classroom. Nevertheless, a growing number of practitioners are assessing its effectiveness (Treisman and Fullilove, 1990; Johnson et al., 1991; Smith et al., 1991; Caprio, 1993; Posner and Markstein, 1994; Cooper, 1995; Watson and Marshall, 1995). While many advocates of collaborative learning are quick to point out its advantages, they are also sensitive to its perceived problems. Cooper (1995), for example, points out that coverage, lack of control during class, and students who do not carry their weight in a group, need to be considered before embarking on collaborative learning. In addition, the evaluation of group work requires careful consideration (see Chapter 6).

LABORATORIES

It is hard to imagine learning to do science, or learning about science, without doing laboratory or field work. Experimentation underlies all scientific knowledge and understanding. Laboratories are wonderful settings for teaching and learning science. They provide students with opportunities to think about, discuss, and solve real problems. Developing and teaching an effective laboratory requires as much skill, creativity, and hard work as proposing and executing a first-rate research project.

Despite the importance of experimentation in science, introductory labs fail to convey the excitement of discovery to the majority of our students. They generally give introductory science labs low marks, often describing them as boring or a waste of time. What is wrong? It is clear that many introductory laboratory programs are suffering from neglect. Typically, students work their way through a list of step-by-step instructions, trying to reproduce expected results and wondering how to get the right answer. While this approach has little do with science, it is common practice because it is efficient. Laboratories are costly and time consuming, and predictable, "cookbook" labs allow departments to offer their lab courses to large numbers of students.

Developing Effective Laboratories

Improving undergraduate laboratory instruction has become a priority in many institutions, driven, in part, by the exciting program being developed at a wide range of institutions. Some labs encourage critical and quantitative thinking, some emphasize demonstration of principles or development of lab techniques, and some help students deepen their understanding of fundamental concepts (Hake, 1992). Where possible, the lab should be coincident with the lecture or discussion. Before you begin to develop a laboratory program, it is important to think about its goals. Here are a number of possibilities:

- Develop intuition and deepen understanding of concepts.
- Apply concepts learned in class to new situations.
- Experience basic phenomena.
- Develop critical, quantitative thinking.
- Develop experimental and data analysis skills.
- Learn to use scientific apparatus.
- Learn to estimate statistical errors and recognize systematic errors.
- Develop reporting skills (written and oral).
- Practice collaborative problem solving.
- Exercise curiosity and creativity by designing a procedure to test a hypothesis.
- Better appreciate the role of experimentation in science.
- Test important laws and rules.

Developing an effective laboratory requires appropriate space and equipment and extraordinary effort from the department's most creative teachers. Still, those who have invested in innovative introductory laboratory programs report very encouraging results: better understanding of the material, much more positive student attitudes toward the lab, and more faculty participation in the lab (Wilson, 1994).

Many science departments have implemented innovative laboratory programs in their introductory courses. We encourage you to consult the organizations and publications listed in the Appendices. Education sessions at professional society meetings are another opportunity to get good ideas for labs in your discipline. Some faculty members have given up lecturing and large

---

Animal Behavior Laboratory at Princeton University

Professor: James L. Gould
Enrollment: approximately 50 students in 3 sections
 A major goal of this course is to teach students how to do science: collect initial observations, formulate testable hypotheses, perform tests, refine or overhaul the original hypothesis, devise a new test, and so on. Each lab is two weeks long, with the equipment and animals available for the entire time. All of the materials that students could plausibly need are stored on shelves for easy and immediate access. In the first hour, we discuss the lab and possible hypotheses, and look over the materials at hand. Each group then formulates an initial plan, obtains approval for their plan, and conducts the experiment.
 The most flexible labs utilize computer-controlled stimuli. In one lab, students are asked to determine to what features of prey a toad responds. Although they begin with live crickets and worms, they are encouraged to use a computer library of "virtual" crickets and toads. Students are given instructions for making new prey models, or modifying existing ones, to test the toad's response to different features. The library includes variations of shape, motion, color, three-dimensionality, size, and so on, plus a variety of cricket chirps and other calls. In general, students quickly discover that virtual crickets work almost as well as real ones—better in that they provide more data since the toad never fills up! A simple statistical program on the computers helps minimize the drudgery of data analysis, enabling the students to concentrate on experimental design and results rather than tedious computations.
 A number of other labs in the course make use of computer-generated and modified stimuli. Labs using this strategy deal with mate recognition in crickets and fish, competitor recognition in fish, predator recognition in chicks and fish, imprinting in ducklings, color change in lizards, and hemispheric dominance in humans.

Cooperative Learning in the Laboratory

Students in two laboratory sections of a chemistry course for non-science majors worked in groups of three on two experiments about acids, bases, and buffers. The experiments were devised using a modified "jigsaw" technique, in which each student in a group is assigned a particular part of a lesson or unit and is responsible for helping the other members of the group learn that material. The week prior to the laboratory, students were given lists of objectives and preparatory work that were divided into three parts. Students decided how to divide the responsibility for the preparatory and laboratory tasks, but were informed that the scores from their post-laboratory exams would be averaged, and that all members of a group would receive the same grade. Two control sections of the same laboratory were conducted in a traditional manner, with students working independently.

All four groups of students were part of the same lecture class, and there were no significant differences in age, gender balance, or previous number of chemistry classes. Although the control sections had an overall GPA higher than the cooperative learning sections (2.77 versus 2.30), the students in the cooperative sections had higher overall scores on the post-lab tests. The authors conclude that use of cooperative learning in the laboratory has a positive effect on student achievement.

Smith et al., 1991.

class meetings in favor of supervised collaborative learning in laboratory settings. Such workshop methods have been devised for teaching physics (Laws, 1991), chemistry (Lisensky et al., 1994), and mathematics (Baxter-Hastings, 1995). Although this is not feasible at many institutions, some of the ideas developed in these courses translate reasonably well to courses in which a lab is associated with a large-enrollment course (Thornton, in press).

Laboratories can be enriched by computers that make data acquisition and analysis easier and much faster, thus allowing students to think about their results and do an improved experiment. Computers can also be used as an element of the experiment to simulate a response, or vary a stimulus. Computers offer convenience, flexibility and safety in the laboratory, but they should not completely replace the student's interaction with the natural world.

Laboratory teaching methods vary widely, but there is certainly no substitute for an instructor circulating among the students, answering and asking questions, pointing out subtle details or possible applications, and generally guiding students' learning. Although students work informally in pairs or groups in many labs, some faculty have formally introduced cooperative learning into their labs (see sidebar). Some instructors rely on a lab handout, not to give cookbook instructions, but to pose a carefully constructed sequence of questions to help students design experiments which illustrate important concepts (Hake, 1992). One advantage of the well-designed handout is that the designer more closely controls what students do in the lab (Moog and Farrell, 1996). The challenge is to design it so that students must think and be creative. In more unstructured labs the challenge is to prevent students from getting stranded and discouraged. Easy access to a faculty member or teaching assistant is essential in this type of lab.

Once you have decided on the goals for your laboratory, and are familiar with some of the innovative ideas in your field, you are ready to ask yourself the following questions:

- How have others operated their programs? Seek out colleagues in other departments or institutions who may have implemented a laboratory program similar to the one you are considering, and learn from their experiences.

- How much time and energy are you willing to invest? Buying new equipment and tinkering with the lab write-ups will probably improve the labs, but much more is required to implement substantial change. Changing the way that students learn involves rethinking the way the lab is taught, writing new lab handouts, setting up a training program for teaching assistants, and perhaps designing some new experiments.
- What support will you have? Solicit the interest and support of departmental colleagues and teaching assistants.
- Are the departmental and institutional administrations supportive of your project and willing to accept the risks? Determine how likely they are to provide the needed resources.
- Are you prepared to go through all of this and still get mediocre student evaluations?

Helping Teaching Assistants to Teach in the Laboratory

- **All teaching assistants perform the laboratory exercises as if they were students to determine operational and analytical difficulties and to test the instructional notes and record-keeping procedures.**
- **Teachers discuss usual student questions and misconceptions and ideas for directing student learning.**
- **Teachers review procedures for circulating among student groups to ensure that each group gets attention. Groups are visited early to help them get started. Each group is visited several other times, but at least midway through the lab to discuss preliminary results and interpretations and toward the end of the lab to review outcomes and interpretations.**
- **Teachers review the students' notebooks or reports and then meet to discuss difficulties and misconceptions. Discussions of grading and comments that might be made are important because these procedures can influence student performance and attitudes on subsequent exercises.**

Lab Reports

The various methods by which students report their lab work have different pedagogical objectives. The formal written report teaches students how to communicate their work in journal style, but students sometimes sacrifice content for appearance. Keeping a lab notebook, which is graded, teaches the student to keep a record while doing an experiment, but it may not develop good writing and presentation skills. Oral reports motivate students to understand their work well enough to explain it to others, but this takes time and does not give students practice in writing. Oral reports can also motivate students to keep a good notebook, especially if they can consult it during their presentation. In choosing this important aspect of the students' lab experience, consider how your students might report their work in the future.

Teaching Labs with Teaching Assistants

Many benefits of carefully planned laboratory exercises are realized only if the instructional staff is well prepared to teach. Often the primary, or only, lab instruction comes from graduate or undergraduate teaching assistants or from faculty members who were not involved in designing the lab. Time must be invested in training the teaching staff, focusing first on their mastery of the lab experiments and then on the method of instruction. It is a fine art to guide students without either simply giving the answer or seeming to be obstinately obscure. Teaching assistants who were not taught in this way can have difficulty adapting to innovative laboratory programs, and the suggestions below will you help you guide their transition. A good part of the success of a course depends on the group spirit of the whole team of instructor and teaching assistants. Many such groups meet weekly, perhaps in an informal but structured way, so that the teaching assistants can provide feedback to the instructor as well as learn about the most effective way to teach the next laboratory experiment (see sidebar).

The responsibility for preparing teaching assistants is largely dependent on the setting. While many faculty members at four-year institutions are responsible for preparing their teaching assistants, this task is handled on a department-wide or campus-wide basis in programs with large numbers of graduate students. Many professional societies have publications on this topic (see Appendix A). The American Association for Higher Education is another excellent source of information. Their publication *Preparing Graduate Students to Teach* (Lambert and Tice, 1993) provides numerous examples of teaching assistant training programs in a wide array of disciplines.

3

Linking Teaching with Learning

- Scientific research as a model of learning and teaching
- Active learning and active teaching

Understanding how students learn can help us develop teaching methods that lead to improvements in students' learning. If our goal is to help our students develop an understanding of science concepts and the scientific enterprise, we need to facilitate students' active involvement in their own learning. As you read this chapter, reflect on your own teaching and think about these questions: What is meant by "active?" How can science inquiry provide a model of effective teaching? What are the basic elements of active teaching and active learning? This chapter presents some practical ideas and methods based on research into human learning. The sidebar at the end of the chapter suggests some additional reading for those who wish to know more than we present here.

A FRAMEWORK FOR LEARNING

Traditionally, college teachers have assumed that students learn through lectures, assigned readings, problem sets, and lab work. Yet we have all been frustrated by the frequent failure of our students to learn basic concepts of science. Because of the pace and large enrollments of many science courses, students are often not able to discuss and reflect on difficult material. Evidence is mounting that these traditional methods are less effective than we once thought in helping our students to develop an understanding of the science concepts that we are teaching (Pearsall, 1992).

People use their experiences to build mental frameworks that help them make sense of the world. Then, when they encounter a strange event or phenomenon, they use these mental frameworks to interpret the information, to make generalizations or to make predictions. The familiar, "Ah ha! Now I get it!" reflects students' active wrestling with a new idea and successful adaptation or modification of mental frameworks. Students, then, are not like blank slates or sponges ready to absorb knowledge. Nor is student performance simply a result of innate ability or of rich experiences, although both affect learning. Rather, experience and knowledge already

Introduction to Physics at Harvard University

Professor: Eric Mazur
Enrollment: Approximately 250 students

In 1989, I read an article in the *American Journal of Physics* that contained a test to assess understanding of Newtonian mechanics. I gave the test to my students at Harvard and was shocked by the results—the students had merely memorized equations and problem-solving procedures and were unable to answer basic questions, indicating a substantial lack of understanding of the material. I began to rethink how I was teaching and realized that students were deriving little benefit from my lectures, even though they generally gave me high marks as a lecturer. So I decided to stop preaching and instead of teaching by telling, I switched to teaching by questioning using a teaching technique I have named "peer instruction."

My students now read the material before class. To get them to do the reading, I begin each class with a short reading quiz. The lecture periods are then broken down into a series of digestible snippets of 10 to 15 minutes. Rather than regurgitating the text, I concentrate on the basic concepts and every 10 or 15 minutes I project a "ConcepTest" on the screen. These short conceptual questions generally require qualitative rather than quantitative answers. The students get one minute to think and choose an answer. They are also expected to record their confidence in their answer. After they record their answers, I ask the students to turn to their neighbors and to convince them of their logic. Chaos erupts as students engage in lively and usually uninhibited discussions of the question. I run up and down the aisles to participate in some of the discussions—to find out how students explain the correct answer in their own words and to find out what mistakes they make.

After one or two minutes, I call time and ask students to record a revised answer and a revised confidence level. A show of hands then quickly reveals the percentage of correct answers. After the discussion, the number of correct answers and the confidence level typically rise dramatically. If I am not satisfied, I repeat the cycle with another question on the same subject. When the results indicate mastery of the concept, I move on to the next subject.

I have been lecturing like this now for more than four years. During this time the students have taught me how best to teach them. As for the students, nothing clarifies their ideas as much as explaining them to others. As one student said in a recent interview: "There is this ah-hah! kind of feeling. It's not that someone just told me; I actually figured it out. And because I can figure it out now, that means I can figure it out on the exam. And I can figure it out for the rest of my life."

acquired affect how students interpret and apply information in new situations (Brooks and Brooks, 1993; Glynn and Duit, 1995).

APPROACHES TO LEARNING

Approaches to and attitudes toward learning vary substantially (Craik and Lockhart, 1972; Witkin and Goodenough, 1981; Koballa, 1995). A student's primary learning style determines how he or she perceives, interacts with, and responds to the learning environment (Claxton and Murrell, 1987; National Center for Improving Science Education, 1991). Thus, teaching methods effective for some students may be ineffective for others. Some students may prefer to have information presented both verbally and graphically, or presented sequentially or hierarchically. Many students learn best through hands-on or personal experience. Some students respond immediately to questions you pose in class while others reflect on possible answers before venturing a response. Some students seem to learn effectively from lectures, while others prefer reading the same material (Tobias, 1992).

Learning is enhanced when we create a classroom environment that provides students with opportunities to learn in several ways. We might, for example, use a graphical display (visual cue) to enhance a lecture (auditory cue). In a genetics lab, we might have students use materials (tactile cue) to make models of DNA. Students might be asked to ride carts around a circular track (kinesthetic cue) to complement vectorial notions of angular momentum.

Whatever the similarities and differences in learning styles and intelligences among our students, we can help all of our students by employing a range of active learning approaches (talking and listening, writing, reading, reflecting) and varied teaching techniques and strategies (such as lectures, videos, demonstrations, discovery labs, collaborative groups, independent projects). Moreover, by using a variety of teaching techniques, we can help students make sense of the world in different ways, increasing the likelihood that they will develop conceptual understanding.

SCIENTIFIC RESEARCH AS A TEACHING AND LEARNING MODEL

Moore (1984) has described science as a "way of knowing," specifically a method that involves disciplined inquiry in the creation of new knowledge. Inquiry—the natural way in which scientists create new knowledge, present it for peer review, and try it out in new settings—can provide a model for how college teaching can likewise become an active process. Scientists and engineers ask questions, and they search for answers by gathering, collating, and interpreting data, weighing risks and benefits, sharing proposed explanations and solutions, and then trying these new proposals out in different contexts. This may raise new questions, and so the process continues in cyclic fashion. Science teaching is often most effective when it captures methods of thinking that scientists use when exploring the world. Successful learning is a complex process that involves more than manipulating symbols or numbers and executing instructions in the laboratory. The activity of finding out can be as important as knowing the answer.

Scientific research involves active investigation of the natural world and social interaction with members of the scientific community. Scientific debates are eventually resolved because the community agrees on what constitutes acceptable evidence, as well as protocols for interpreting that evidence. Similarly, science learning must be an interactive process in which students become engaged with scientific phenomena and debate with both peers and instructors in order to develop a full understanding of related phenomena and underlying concepts. When we teach science only as a set of truths, we run the risk of subverting our students' attempts to grapple with problems and make new experiences meaningful. We deny them the opportunity to engage in the scientific process.

While science understanding comes through an individual's personal efforts at making sense of the world around him or her, not all knowledge can come through individual discovery. Indeed, a good deal of our science knowledge must come from lectures, texts, and original sources. How might you, as a teacher, make better use of traditional formats to help your students gain knowledge *and understanding?* The sections that follow provide a sequence for teaching and learning that incorporates four basic elements used by research scientists.

Engaging Students

Scientists embark upon a problem because they have had their curiosity piqued by a strange event or a puzzling question or some other occurrence that causes them to wonder and resolve the apparent discrepancy between what they know and what they are experiencing. Similarly, instructors can help students become active learners by motivating them with open-ended questions, puzzles, and paradoxes. What happens when. . . ? Why does that happen? But how can that be, when we know that. . . ?

Full integration of new knowledge is enhanced by time to reflect. Reflection is especially beneficial immediately following the presentation of new, challenging material. One effective method (Rowe, 1974) is to provide, after ten minutes of lecturing, short periods (a minute or two) for students to think. The necessary structure can be provided by a pertinent question.

An alternative to asking questions is to ask students to summarize some important ideas from a previous discussion or the reading assignment. This focuses their attention and gives the teacher an opportunity to assess their level of understanding. Because students' disposition to learn can be influenced by the knowledge or mental frameworks they bring to class, assessing for prior knowledge is an essential component of teaching for active learning. As we shall see in the next chapter, students often approach learning situations with misconceptions or with prior knowledge that actually impedes learning. Students are most likely to change their beliefs if they first develop dissatisfaction with those beliefs and recognize possible alternatives as they prepare themselves to adopt a new, more acceptable view (Anderson and Roth, 1992; Minstrell, 1989; Posner et al., 1982; West and Pines, 1985). Stepans (1994) has summarized major physical science misconceptions and developed a suggested teaching sequence based on Posner's research for helping students confront these ideas. His model of teaching is parallel to the way scientists conduct research and how they resolve discrepancies between their current views and new information they are encountering.

Establishing a Context for Exploration

Just as a scientist explores various possibilities for resolving differences between the current view of a subject and new and contradictory information, so too does a teacher have to provide students with a chance to explore their ideas. This could be a laboratory experiment that helps students take the first step in finding answers to the questions posed in lecture or in class. Informal investigation, whether it occurs in the laboratory, in small group discussion sessions, or during a search of the World Wide Web, gives students firsthand exposure to inquiry.

Students need to talk with peers and their teacher in order to articulate what they have experienced during these explorations. Talking helps students work through their preliminary thoughts about a concept. Some structure and guidelines can help students find a forum to discuss and clarify their thinking. You might ask students to form small groups in order to work on problems and discuss major concepts, for example, those which relate to the lab experiment.

Thinking Aloud Pair Problem Solving (TAPPS)

A technique called "thinking aloud pair problem solving" (TAPPS) can help students apply difficult concepts. One student of the pair attempts to solve a problem while the other listens and tries to clarify what is being said. Thinking aloud works because it makes students aware of their thought processes as they solve problems; it also helps them quickly see when they make errors or turn into blind alleys (Whimbey, 1986).

Posing Questions about Reading Assignments

Many introductory science texts contain discussion questions at the end of each chapter. Some faculty ask students to consider these questions while they read the chapter, rather than when they have finished it, in order to focus on key ideas. Although some of the questions simply require students to locate factual information, those which go beyond basic definitions (e.g., "Where do you run into this term in your everyday experience?") or which ask the student to think critically about the factual information (e.g., "What does it mean to say the periodic table was useful because it 'worked'? How does this relate to the scientific method?") are better suited for use as the student reads the chapter.

Questions: Trefil and Hazen, 1995.

Learning to Write a Research Paper

A practical writing exercise for science majors in advanced courses is to write up an experiment as though they were submitting it to a professional journal. Students do the lab work in the usual way, up to the data collection. However, instead of writing a standard lab report or summary in their lab notebook, they are required to identify an appropriate journal and follow its rules for submission. Presentation of experimental data, figures, conclusions, and references must conform to the submission guidelines. Similar to journal submissions, students' papers may require several revisions before they are "published" (i.e., receive a final grade). You can use this reporting method to help students improve their writing and presentation skills as well as to think more deeply about one or more of their experiments. Although it is more work, students view the "paper" report as a valuable and practical experience.

Proposing Explanations

Having interested your students in describing and exploring some phenomena, you might provide opportunities for them to attempt explanations and synthesis. Again, you might use leading questions: Can anyone suggest, in your own words, an explanation for A? Does that idea also explain B? Can anyone think of a counterexample?

As teachers, we know that one of the best ways to learn something is to explain it to someone else. You can give your students this experience by asking them to write a short summary paper addressed to a non-scientist in which they attempt to clarify difficult concepts like mass, molecule, or homeostasis. This exercise helps students understand new concepts as they connect their current knowledge with recently learned information. Explanatory writing requires students to organize their thoughts as they plan how to explain something to a peer who is not familiar with the concept. As Meyers and Jones (1993) recognize, ". . . writing can be a powerful prod to the expansion, modification and creation of mental structures."

Reading and Writing for Understanding

Students can solidify their understanding of a science concept by applying their explanation in a new setting. This process helps students create new mental frameworks that lead to deeper understanding. Opportunities for reading and reflection can also help students incorporate new concepts. We know from studies of reading with secondary students that giving specific study questions before students start reading increases the likelihood that students will recall the information they read (Winograd and Newell, 1984). Thus, by giving explicit instructions for an assigned reading, you can increase what students comprehend in the reading.

There are a number of ways to encourage students to reflect on their learning by writing about it. Some college teachers have found that journals are a useful learning tool for college students. Students need not write every day, but frequent writing in which students reflect critically on a lecture, a lab, or a text assignment and integrate these components of a course helps them make sense of the complex conceptual ideas of science (Bonwell and Eison, 1991). In many ways, this process is similar to keeping a research notebook, in which you summarize and reflect critically on one or more completed experiments and begin to make connections between their outcomes.

Selected Resources on How Students Learn

This list is not comprehensive, but aims to provide a starting point for those seeking additional reading on this topic.

A fuller discussion of the active mind and the structured mind in learning:

Gelman, R. and M. G. Lee. 1995. Trends and Developments in Educational Psychology in the United States. New York: UNESCO.

A fuller discussion of how different representational systems are at work during learning:

Copple, C. E., I. E. Sigel, and R. Saunders. 1984. Educating the Young Thinker. Hillsdale, N.J.: Lawrence Erlbaum and Associates.

Interesting readings about the active processes of discovery among scientists as they engage in problem solving in their laboratories:

Dunbar, K. 1995. How scientists really reason: Scientific reasoning in real-world laboratories. In R. J. Stern and J. Davidson, eds. Mechanisms of Insight. Cambridge, Mass.: MIT Press.

Dunbar, K. 1996. How scientists think: Online creativity and conceptual change in science. In T. B. Ward, S. M. Smith, and S. Vaid, eds. Conceptual Structures and Processes: Emergence, Discovery, and Change. Washington, D.C.: APA Press.

Building on the active learning work by Gelman and Lee cited earlier in this sidebar, this paper emphasizes discovery processes in which learners engage, and suggests ways that teachers can facilitate this kind of learning:

Schauble, L. 1996. The development of scientific reasoning in knowledge-rich contexts. Developmental Psychology 32:102-119.

For further reading on teacher-student collaboration in building knowledge frameworks:

Schauble, L., R. Glaser, R. A. Duschl, S. Schulze, and J. John. 1995. Students' understanding of the objectives and procedures of the experimentation in the science classroom. Journal of the Learning Sciences 4(2):131-166.

For further reading about building a community of learners:

Brown, A. L. 1994. The advancement of learning. Educational Researcher 23(8):4-12.

4

Misconceptions as Barriers to Understanding Science

- The role of misconceptions in the learning process
- Descriptions and examples of some common misconceptions in science
- Methods to identify misconceptions
- Methods to break down misconceptions

Teachers can be astonished to learn that despite their best efforts, students do not grasp fundamental ideas covered in class. Even some of the best students give the right answers but are only using correctly memorized words. When questioned more closely, these students reveal their failure to understand fully the underlying concepts. Students are often able to use algorithms to solve numerical problems without completely understanding the underlying scientific concept. Mazur (1996) reports that students in his physics class had memorized equations and problem-solving skills, but performed poorly on tests of conceptual understanding. Nakhleh and Mitchell (1993) studied sixty students in an introductory course for chemistry majors. In an exam which paired an algorithmic problem with a conceptual question on the same topic, only 49% of those students classified as having high algorithmic ability were able to answer the parallel conceptual question.

Besides offering students information and helpful examples, we must show them the reasoning processes that lead to algorithms and conceptual generalizations. Inclusion of conceptual questions on tests is another way to emphasize the importance of this aspect of problem solving (see Chapter 6). In many cases students have developed partially correct ideas that can be used as the foundation for further learning (Clement et al., 1989). However, many students have not developed an appropriate understanding of fundamental concepts from the beginning of their studies, and this shortcoming can interfere with subsequent learning.

TYPES OF MISCONCEPTIONS

A familiar example from elementary school is students' understanding of the relationship between the earth and the sun. While growing up, children are told by adults that the "sun is rising and setting," giving them an image of a sun that moves about the earth. In school, students are told by teachers (years after they have already formed their own mental model of how things work) that the earth rotates. Students are then faced with the difficult task of deleting a mental image that makes sense to them, based on their own observations, and replacing it with a model that is not as intuitively acceptable. This task is not trivial, for students must undo a whole mental framework of knowledge that they have used to understand the world.

The example of the earth rotating rather than the sun orbiting the earth is one of many that teachers refer to collectively as misconceptions. Misconceptions can be categorized as follows:

- *Preconceived notions* are popular conceptions rooted in everyday experiences. For example, many people believe that water flowing underground must flow in streams because the water they see at the earth's surface flows in streams. Preconceived notions plague students' views of heat, energy, and gravity (Brown and Clement, 1991), among others.

- *Nonscientific beliefs* include views learned by students from sources other than scientific education, such as religious or mythical teachings. For example, some students have learned through religious instruction about an abbreviated history of the earth and its life forms. The disparity between this widely held belief and the scientific evidence for a far more extended pre-history has led to considerable controversy in the teaching of science.

- *Conceptual misunderstandings* arise when students are taught scientific information in a way that does not provoke them to confront paradoxes and conflicts resulting from their own preconceived notions and nonscientific beliefs. To deal with their confusion, students construct faulty models that usually are so weak that the students themselves are insecure about the concepts.

- *Vernacular misconceptions* arise from the use of words that mean one thing in everyday life and another in a scientific context (e.g., "work"). A geology professor noted that students have difficulty with the idea that glaciers retreat, because they picture the glacier stopping, turning around, and moving in the opposite direction. Substitution of the word "melt" for "retreat" helps reinforce the correct interpretation that the front end of the glacier simply melts faster than the ice advances.

- *Factual misconceptions* are falsities often learned at an early age and retained unchallenged into adulthood. If you think about it, the idea that "lightning never strikes twice in the same place" is clearly nonsense, but that notion may be buried somewhere in your belief system. (See the sidebar for another example.)

HOW TO BREAK DOWN MISCONCEPTIONS

Although vernacular and factual misconceptions can often be easily corrected, even by the students themselves, it is not effective for a teacher simply to insist that the learner dismiss preconceived notions and ingrained nonscientific beliefs. Recent research on students' conceptual misunderstandings of natural phenomena indicates that new concepts cannot be learned if alternative models that explain a phenomenon already exist in the learner's mind. Although scientists commonly view such erroneous models with disdain, they are often preferred by the learner because they seem more reasonable and perhaps are more useful for the learner's purpose (Mayer, 1987). These beliefs can persist as lingering suspicions in a student's mind and can hinder further learning (McDermott, 1991).

Before embracing the concepts held to be correct by the scientific community, students must confront their own beliefs along with their associated paradoxes and limitations and then attempt to reconstruct the knowledge necessary to understand the scientific model being presented. This process requires that the teacher:

- Identify students' misconceptions.
- Provide a forum for students to confront their misconceptions.
- Help students reconstruct and internalize their knowledge, based on scientific models.

These steps are discussed throughout the remainder of this chapter.

Identifying Misconceptions

Before misconceptions can be corrected, they need to be identified. Many researchers and teachers have compiled lists of commonly encountered misconceptions (see sidebar at the end of the chapter). A number of professional societies have developed conceptual tests which allow you to identify students' misconceptions; we urge you to consult the organizations in Appendix B for more information. Additionally, small group discussions and office hours provide effective forums for identifying student misconceptions. With practice and effort, a teacher can learn to probe a student's conceptual framework (often by simply listening) without resorting to authority or embarrassing the student. Mazur has found a way to help students check their conceptual frameworks even within the large lecture format (see the sidebar in Chapter 3). Hake (1992) has used introductory laboratory exercises to help students test their conceptual bases for understanding motion. Essay assignments that ask students to explain their reasoning are useful for detecting students' misconceptions. These essays and discussions need not be used for grading, but rather can be used as part of the learning process to find out what and how your students are thinking.

Misconceptions can occur in students' understanding of scientific methods as well as in their organization of scientific knowledge. For example, students in a science class will often express disappointment that an experiment did not work. They do not fully understand that experiments are a means of testing ideas and hypotheses, not of arriving at an expected result. To the scientist, an experiment yields a result which needs to be interpreted. In that sense, each experiment "works," but it may not work as expected.

Helping Students Confront Their Misconceptions

It is useful to review and think about possible misconceptions before teaching a class or laboratory in which new ma-

Example of a Factual Misconception

A grade-school geography teacher once informed my whole class that the Gulf Stream is simply and entirely the Mississippi River, floating across the surface of the salty Atlantic all the way to Norway. I duly learned that, and never thought about it again. It sat unexamined and unchallenged in my head for several decades, until the subject arose in a discussion with colleagues, and up it came like some weird deep-sea fish; I had only to mention it to be roundly hooted (by myself as well after giving it a half-second's thought). I was impressed by the clarity and circumstantial detail with which that fragile "unfact" was preserved for decades in my head; I bet there are others, and I bet we all have them. There may be families of them, lurking like coelacanths in the collective depths. I know there are twenty or thirty of us out there who either have dredged up and exploded the Gulf Stream heresy, or are still carrying it around intact (Blackburn, 1995).

terial is introduced. Use questions and discussion to probe for additional misconceptions. Students will often surprise you with the variety of their preconceptions, so be careful to listen closely to their answers and explanations. You can help students by asking them to give evidence to support their explanations and by revisiting difficult or misunderstood concepts after a few days or weeks. Misconceptions are often deeply held, largely unexplained, and sometimes strongly defended. To be effective, a science teacher should not underestimate the importance and the persistence of these barriers to true understanding. Confronting them is difficult for the student and the teacher.

Some misconceptions can be uncovered by asking students to sketch or describe some object or phenomenon. For example, one might ask students to sketch an atom before doing so on the board. Even students who have a strong high school background might show a small nucleus surrounded by many electrons circling in discrete orbital paths, much like the solar system. By asking them to draw their own model first and then asking some students to share their answers with the class, a teacher can identify preexisting models and use them to show the need for new models.

Example of a Conceptual Misunderstanding

Students were asked to sketch the air in a sealed flask initially and after half of the air was removed. In this study, fifteen percent of college chemistry students sketched the second flask with regions containing air and other regions containing empty space (Benson et al., 1993).

Helping Students Overcome Their Misconceptions

Strategies for helping students to overcome their misconceptions are based on research about how we learn (Arons, 1990; Minstrell, 1989). The key to success is ensuring that students are constructing or reconstructing a correct framework for their new knowledge. One way of establishing this framework is to have students create "concept maps," an approach pioneered by Novak and Gowin (1984). With this technique, students learn to visualize a group of concepts and their interrelationships. Boxes containing nouns (and sometimes adjectives) are connected to related terms with a series of lines; prepositions or verbs are superimposed on the connecting lines to help clarify the relationship. A sample concept map is shown in Figure 4.1 While some studies indicate that concept maps do not enhance meaningful learning in biology (Lehman et al., 1985), others have obtained the opposite result (Okebukola and Jegede, 1988). Esiobu and Soyibo (1995) reported that students constructing concept maps in cooperative groups show a greater increase in conceptual learning than students working individually, thus the utility of concept mapping may depend on the instructional setting. Similar results were obtained by Basili and Sanford (1991), who found that cooperative group work on concept-focused tasks had a significant effect in helping college students overcome certain misconceptions in chemistry, even though it did not involve concept maps.

Using Demonstrations to Help Students Overcome Misconceptions

Carefully selected demonstrations are one way of helping students overcome misconceptions, and there are a variety of resources available (Katz, 1991). In the example of a conceptual misunderstanding about gas volume cited in an earlier sidebar, the authors suggest that a demonstration using a colored gas could be very effective in showing students that the gas fills its container.

Helping students to reconstruct their conceptual framework is a difficult task, and it necessarily takes time away from other activities in a science course. However, if you decide to make the effort to help students overcome their misconceptions you might try the following methods:

- Anticipate the most common misconceptions about the material and be alert for others.
- Encourage students to test their conceptual frameworks in discussion with other students and by thinking about the evidence and possible tests.
- Think about how to address common misconceptions with demonstrations and lab work.
- Revisit common misconceptions as often as you can.
- Assess and reassess the validity of student concepts.

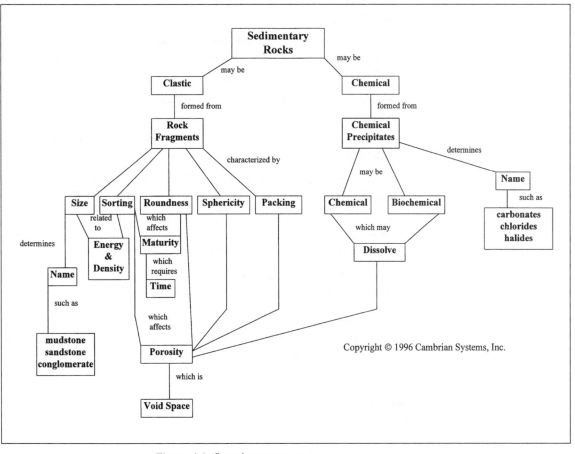

Figure 4.1. Sample concept map

Selected Resources on Misconceptions

This list is not intended to be comprehensive, but instead aims to provide a starting point for those seeking additional reading on this topic.

Cho, H., J. B. Kahle, and F. H. Nordland. 1985. An investigation of high school biology textbooks as sources of misconceptions and difficulties in genetics and some suggestions for teaching genetics. Sci. Educ. 69(5):707-719.

Lawson, A. E. and L. D. Thompson. 1988. Formal reasoning ability and misconceptions concerning genetics and natural selection. J. Res. Sci. Teaching 25(9):733-746.

Nakhleh, M. B. 1992. Why some students don't learn chemistry. J. Chem. Educ. 69(3):191-196.

Novak, J. D., ed. 1987. Proceedings of the Second International Seminar on Misconceptions and Educational Strategies in Science and Mathematics. Ithaca, N. Y.:Cornell University.

Peters, P. 1982. Even honors students have conceptual difficulties with physics. Am. J. Physics 50:501-508.

A Private Universe. 1989. Cambridge, Mass.: Harvard-Smithsonian Center for Astrophysics.

Trowbridge, J. E. and J. J. Mintzes. 1988. Alternative conception in animal classification: a cross-age study. J. Res. Sci. Teaching 25(7):547-561.

Wandersee, J. H., J. J. Mintzes, and J. D. Novak. 1994. Research on alternative conceptions in science. In Handbook of Research on Science Teaching and Learning, pp. 177-210. D. Gabel, ed. New York: MacMillan.

Zoller, U. 1990. Students' misunderstandings and misconceptions in college freshman chemistry. J. Res. Sci. Teaching. 27(10):1053-1065.

A bibliography of some 3,500 published items called Students' Alternative Frameworks in Science is available on-line in two parts (introduction and database) and can be downloaded anonymously from an FTP server.
host: topgun.idbsu.edu
user id: anonymous
password: your e-mail address
directory: physlrnr

Download files "plr11" (the intro, about 25 KB) and "plr12" (the database, about 700 KB). There are two versions of each, one in Word 5.1 for Mac suffixed "mac.bin" and another for pc in Word for Windows 2.0 suffixed "pc.doc."

Dykstra, D. I., Jr. 1995. From email discussion list posted to cur-l@listserv.ncsu.edu on Feb. 15, 1995, subject Scientific misunderstandings, by David Houseman. The archive for this list is located at listserv@ncsu.edu.

5

Evaluation of Teaching and Learning

- Obtaining frequent feedback on your teaching
- Getting regular insight on student learning
- Soliciting student opinion during the term
- Assessing a course at the end of the term

Educational researchers have found that effective teachers share several characteristics (e.g., Angelo and Cross, 1993; Davis, 1993; Murray, 1991; Reynolds, 1992; Shulman, 1990). Two of these characteristics stand out:

- Through frequent assessment and feedback, effective teachers regularly assess what they do in the classroom and whether their students are really learning.
- They try to anticipate the topics and concepts that will be difficult for their students and to develop teaching strategies that present these topics in ways their students will best understand. These teachers make a special point of becoming familiar with their students' preparation, knowledge, and abilities, and adjust their teaching to maximize the class's learning.

Yet, teachers, especially new teachers, may sometimes be too overwhelmed by all that is involved with teaching to assess student knowledge and learning. Creating a syllabus, preparing assignments, developing lectures, designing laboratories, structuring discussions, and writing test questions all take time, thought, and planning. The following sections describe various assessment schemes for both you and your students.

DETERMINING WHAT STUDENTS KNOW

Learning science is a cumulative process; each new piece of information is added to what students already know (or believe) about the topic at hand. If students have a solid foundation, the new pieces fit together more easily. However, if the students' preparation is spotty or incomplete, they may find it harder to grasp the new material. If the new material conflicts with earlier misconceptions or firmly held assumptions, the students unfortunately may ignore or distort the new information so that it fits into their old framework of understanding (American Psychological Association, 1992; Pintrich, 1988; see also Chapter 4). This suggests the following:

- At the beginning of every course, try to gauge the students' prior knowledge of the subject. What are the prerequisites for your course, and have all student taken the prerequisites? There are several ways to identify what students already know (Davis, 1993; Angelo and Cross, 1993); one of the simplest is introduce a topic and then ask a question which brings out their knowledge such as "What's going on here? How do we know that?" If student answers are recorded, the same questions can be posed again at the end of the topic or term to evaluate students' progress.

- A more comprehensive way to learn about students' prior knowledge is to give a brief diagnostic pretest—ungraded and anonymous. The diagnostic pretest might include a list of key concepts, facts and figures, or major ideas. Ask students to indicate their familiarity with each topic.

- During the term, frequent diagnostic mini-quizzes can help identify which students are keeping up and which need help. These quizzes also help students to identify the areas on which they need to work. Reading the quizzes will give the instructor a good indication of where to start the next class.

Are Students Learning What You Are Teaching?

Most undergraduate courses include students with a range of academic abilities, interests, skills, and goals. Differences in preparation, abilities, and learning styles are likely to be more noticeable when new information is abstract and complex. Individual students do not make uniform progress; sometimes a student reaches a plateau after a burst of learning. Try to sample how well your students are learning. Typically, when teachers want to assess students' learning, they tend first to think of giving tests or quizzes; however, there are alternatives to the standard test or quiz. Informal ways can be used to determine whether students are learning the material throughout the term. Some suggestions (see, for example, Davis 1993; Silberman, 1996) to try are to:

- Ask questions during class. Give the students time to respond. Try to get a sense of whether students are keeping up by asking questions for which answers require students to apply a given concept or skill to a new context.

- Ask students for their questions. Rather than ask, "Do you have any questions?," ask instead "What questions do you have?" This implies that you expect questions and are encouraging students to ask them.

- Give frequent, short, in-class assignments or quizzes. Pose a question or problem on an overhead or the board, give students time to respond, perhaps in writing, and have students compare answers with their neighbors. Open-ended questions such as "How does food give us energy?" "What does it mean when we say a battery is dead?" or "Which light bulb will be the brightest, and why?" are but a few examples.

- Ask students to write a "minute paper." Just before the end of a class session, ask: "What is the most significant thing you learned today?" and, perhaps in addition, "What question is uppermost in your mind at the end of today's class?" These "minute papers" should be collected as students leave class. Reading these will help you to evaluate how well your students are grasping the material, and you can respond, if needed, during the next class period.
- Ask students to jot down three or four key concepts or real-world connections about a recent topic, then start a class discussion by having students compare their lists.
- Ask students to keep a learning journal in which they write, once or twice a week, about things they disagree with or how what they are learning is reflected in other things they read, see, or do. Collect and comment on the learning journals periodically.

ASSESSING YOUR COURSE

It is common practice to wait until the end of the term to ask students how successful the course has been. An alternative approach is to request informal constructive criticism throughout the term, when classroom presentations, organization, pacing, and workload can be adjusted. Instructors can gather information about the effectiveness of their teaching strategies, the usefulness of instructional materials, and other features of the course (e.g., the turnaround time on exams and assignments or number of problems assigned as homework) that can be changed during the semester.

Soliciting Students' Opinions About Your Course

It is a good idea for faculty who are teaching a course for the first time or who have significantly revised a course to solicit feedback from students soon after the term begins. Faculty who are teaching a course they have taught many times before may want to wait until midterm before asking for student assessments, although if feedback is solicited immediately after an exam, most of the comments will relate to the exam. If your students are having obvious difficulties with the material or with other requirements, try to find out why, using some of the quick techniques mentioned earlier. Many teachers now use electronic mail. Give students your e-mail address and ask them to mail questions, concerns, or comments about the course (see Chapter 7 for more ideas). Other faculty find it helpful to ask, after the first month, that students bring a sheet, which can be anonymous, with their answer to the question: "How are you getting along in this course? Any suggestions?" This free-form feedback, of the most varied sort, can be extremely valuable in diagnosing what is getting across or whether the pace is right. However, at some institutions, feedback during the term must be anonymous, to minimize any perception that a student's comments influenced his or her grade. In this situation, you might ask a colleague to collect the comments and summarize them for you.

Some faculty members feel awkward soliciting feedback and reporting back to the class. Many find it helpful first to look over the positive things students have said about the course (this step is reassuring and puts the negative comments in perspective). Then they consider the suggestions for improvement and group them into three categories: those that can be changed this term (e.g., the turnaround time on lab assignments), those that need to wait until the next time the course is offered (e.g., the textbook), and those that cannot, for pedagogical or other reasons, be changed (e.g., content required for subsequent courses). Other ways to respond to advice:

- From time to time restate and clarify the course's goals and expectations. If changes are to be made, give a brief account of which changes will be made this term and which will be used in future courses.
- Let students know what they can do as well. For example, if students report that they are often confused, invite them to ask questions more often.
- Consider making changes to your course or teaching methods based upon the feedback.

Using a Portfolio to Assess Your Course

Faculty members at some colleges and universities are beginning to experiment with teaching portfolios composed of work samples and self-evaluative commentary. A portfolio might include copies of syllabi, assignments, handouts, and teaching notes; copies of students' lab notebooks or assignments; descriptions of steps taken to evaluate and improve one's teaching (such as exchanging course materials with colleagues or using fast-feedback techniques); and information from students (such as student rating forms). Portfolios can also include a statement of your teaching philosophy. Advice on how to put together a portfolio can be found in Edgerton et al. (1991) and Urbach (1992). Less comprehensive than portfolios are self-evaluations that ask faculty to comment on their courses: How satisfied were you with this course? What do you think were the strong points of the course and your teaching? The weak points? What did you find most interesting about this course? Most frustrating? What would you do differently if you taught this course again?

HOW WELL ARE YOU TEACHING?

In addition to evaluating your course using the fast feedback methods or teaching portfolio described above, other powerful methods for evaluating your teaching include formal end-of-term student evaluations, peer review, and videotaping.

Watching Yourself on Videotape

- **What are the specific things I did well?**
- **What are the specific things I could have done better?**
- **What kept the students engaged?**
- **When did students get lost or lose interest?**
- **If I could do this session over again, what three things would I change?**
- **How would I go about making those changes?**

Evaluating Your Own Teaching

Videotaping is one way to view and listen to the class as your students do; you can also observe your students' reactions and responses to your teaching. You can also check the accuracy of your perceptions of how well you teach and identify those techniques that work and those that need improvement. Many schools have professional development offices which can help with taping or assessing the tapes, but informal recording by the instructor can be useful and effective. However, you may want someone from the professional development office to view the tape with you to avoid focusing on your appearance or mannerisms. An experienced evaluator

Conducting Effective Classroom Observations

Successful peer review programs which include classroom visits share a number of features. These programs work best when faculty members:

- Use a team or partner approach, in which faculty pair up or work in small groups to visit one another's classes.
- Conduct visits as part of a consultation process that involves a pre-visit conference to discuss goals for the class, and a post-visit debriefing to discuss what happened.
- Combine classroom observation with other strategies that enrich the picture such as interviewing students, reviewing materials, and examining student work.
- Are self-conscious about the learning that can occur for the observer as well as the observed.
- Let the students know what is happening, and why.
- Are purposeful about who might best visit whom. Depending on their questions and purposes, they may want to pair up with someone from the same field who can comment on content; alternatively, if they are experimenting with a new teaching strategy, they might want to find a colleague who has extensive experience with that strategy.
- Keep track of how classroom observation is working, so they can learn from the process and improve it.

Hutchings, 1996.

can help you focus on those aspects of your teaching that influence its effectiveness (Davis, 1993).

How can you analyze your classroom interactions with students? As you watch the tape, try the technique of stopping every five seconds and putting a check in the following columns: teacher talk, student talk, silence. Or look at your lecture in terms of organization and preparation: Did I give the purpose of the session? Emphasize or restate the most important ideas? Make smooth transitions from one topic to another? Summarize the main points? Include neither too much nor too little material in a class period? Seem at ease with the material? Begin and end class promptly?

Peer Evaluation of Your Teaching

Peer review of one's research results is standard practice in all fields of science, but only recently has this become a mechanism for advancing one's teaching knowledge and skills. The American Association for Higher Education has shown leadership in this area through its "Peer Review of Teaching" project (Hutchings, 1996). Although conceived as an effort to improve the quality of evidence about teaching in faculty tenure and promotion decisions, the project puts greater emphasis on faculty collaboration to improve teaching throughout their careers. Reciprocal classroom visits, mentoring programs for new faculty, team teaching, and departmental seminars about teaching and learning are but a few of the ways that faculty members work with colleagues to improve undergraduate education.

Students' Evaluation of Your Teaching

The most common way to evaluate a course and a faculty member's teaching is to use a student rating form at the end of the term. These forms often are used by faculty committees and administrators to make personnel decisions about merit increases, promotion, and tenure for faculty. A substantial body of research has concluded that administering questionnaires to students can be both valid and reliable, providing faculty and administrators with a wealth of knowledge about the attitudes, behavior, and values of students (Hinton, 1993). Advice on how to design, administer, and interpret evaluation forms can be found in Cashin (1990), Theall and Franklin (1990), Davis (1993), and Braskamp and Ory (1994).

Despite their widespread use, there is no clear consensus on the connection between students' learning and their rating of the instructor. Some studies suggest that student ratings of the instructor's teaching correlate somewhat with student learning (Marsh and Dunkin, 1992). However, Arons (1990) observes that many vacuous courses in science have been developed which students have rated highly, describing them as fun and exciting. Subsequent testing indicated that these students learned very little. This does not suggest that student perspectives are unimportant. However, before distributing the evaluation forms, many instructors tell students the purpose of the forms. When students know how the forms will be used, and are confident that their comments will be taken seriously, faculty are more likely to receive evaluations that can help them improve their teaching and their course.

6

Testing and Grading

- Ways to assess student learning
- Goals for tests
- Suggestions to help students do better on exams
- Descriptions of common testing methods
- Issues to consider when assigning test grades

In addition to the informal assessments described in Chapter 5, more formal assessments of student progress provide important gauges of student learning. At most institutions, testing students and assigning them grades provide the bases for such evaluations. Grading practices in a course can both motivate students and define the goals of a course. Grades may influence students' decisions to select a field as a major or a career (Seymour and Hewitt, 1994). Although a course may offer many activities and learning opportunities, faculty members declare what is important in their courses by their decisions of what to grade, how to test, and how much a particular score counts toward the final grade. Students who measure their learning by the grade they receive tend to invest time only in aspects of a course that clearly affect their grade.

Aspects of a course that may be part of a final grade include tests, weekly problem assignments, oral or written reports, library research projects, essays, group projects, and laboratory performance. For each activity, students deserve to know how they will be graded, and they deserve careful, detailed, and timely comments on their performance. For each aspect of your course, try to identify the important skills, learning, and accomplishments you hope to measure, then determine how to grade them fairly and equitably.

GRADING SPECIFIC ACTIVITIES

Laboratory activities involve aspects of reasoning, teamwork, experimental design, data acquisition and recording, data analysis, discussion, interpretation, and reporting. One way of grading labs (Kandel, 1989; Joshi, 1991) is to assess the following:

39

- Understanding the results, whether or not they agree with expectations.
- Decision-making skills based on results both expected and unanticipated (application of theory).
- Method of recording, presenting, and analyzing data; observations and results (the notebook and final report).
- Performance of physical manipulations (technique).

Rondini and Feighan (1978) describe a chemistry lab in which they give students at the end of each lab a numerical score for specific attributes, such as the product yield, equipment setup, handling of chemicals, purity of product, time to completion, technique, safety procedures. These scores are added to the grades for their lab reports and notebooks. Thus, students know quickly what aspects of their lab techniques need improvement and can use this information as a catalyst for change. Joshi (1991) asks students to prepare and submit their lab reports on-line. The computer checks and grades the quality of input data; performs and displays the necessary calculations; checks and grades students' calculations and accuracy of the results; generates a grade report; and displays the grading scheme used.

When assigning *essays or written reports* as activities for grading, explain to students the important aspects of the assignment and describe how it will be graded. One might include content, research, references, reasoning, data analysis and clear expression (see sidebar for an example). Another aid to student learning is to grade first drafts and give students a chance to resubmit an improved version. If instructor time is a significant deterrent to this approach, students can exchange draft reports with a partner or gather in a group and critique one another's drafts.

Oral reports and presentations can be difficult to grade, especially when students have little experience with this skill. It can be hard to overlook poor delivery and focus on content. Some faculty members develop a scoring rubric that weight these two components unequally, and which give credit for effective use of visuals. When students do more than one presentation in a term, the weight given to delivery is increased to reflect the expectation that they will have improved with experience.

Group activities are difficult to grade on an individual basis. Most instructors find that a good way to grade a group is to make the entire group responsible for the answers, presentation, and results, by giving each group member the same grade. This encourages stronger students to help less able students. Observing the groups in action will give you an idea of how each participant performs as a partner. Students are also quite cognizant of their contribution and their fellow classmates' contribution. One approach is to ask students to estimate the percentage of the final project that can be attributed to each group member, including themselves. You can use these ratings from all members to construct a participation score, so that there are slight differences when one group member contributes significantly more or less than the others. Some recommend that group activity grades account for only a small portion of a student's overall grade in the class (Johnson et al., 1991).

You will need to decide how to address *homework problems*, if you feel that these are an important aspect of student learning. If you choose not to collect and grade them, many students will interpret that as a signal that you do not consider them important. However, some faculty get around this problem by duplicating some of the assigned problems on their tests. If you choose to make homework a part of the final course grade, you need to

Grading Students' Essays

The English department at Dickinson College conducts a seminar for faculty teaching in the Freshman Seminar program, to help them learn to teach writing to new students and to evaluate students' assignments. They suggest assigning a percentage to the various categories shown below, with approximately equal weight given to content and presentation. When students hand in a rough draft, they recommend assigning it a nominal percentage, and grading it on the basis of whether the student has made reasonable progress on the assignment. The grade sheet typically occupies a full page, with adequate space left for instructor comments. A sample grading sheet is shown.

Evaluation of Paper #1

__Quality of effort on draft = 10%__

Score: _____

__Content = 40%__   Score: _____
1. Paper responds to the assignment
2. Focuses on central idea or thesis
3. Thesis supported by evidence

__Organization = 25%__   Score: _____
1. Paper has an introduction, development, and conclusion
2. Paragraphs coherent and focused on single idea
3. Paragraphs are related to central thesis
4. Transitions between paragraphs are logical, so that the reader can follow the development of the thesis

__Mechanics = 15%__   Score: _____
1. Sentence structure
2. Word usage
3. Punctuation
4. Spelling

__Style = 10%__   Score: _____
1. Sentences varied and not awkward
2. Language is uninflated and appropriate for a formal paper (no slang, contractions, etc.)

Paper 1 grade: _____

make a number of decisions. What percentage of the overall grade should it be? Will students work alone or in groups? Will they submit individual papers or a single answer set for the group?

THE WHY AND HOW OF TESTS

Ideally, tests measure students' achievement of the educational goals for the course, and the test items sample the content and skills that are most important for students to learn. Tests usually ask students questions about material that is most essential to the discipline. A well-constructed test measures a range of cognitive skills, not just students' recall of facts. However, it is unlikely "that research will ever demonstrate clearly which form of examination, essay or objective, has the more beneficial influence on study and learning" (Ebel and Frisbie, 1986). Your choice of examination form will need to take into account many factors such as the time available for students to take the test, the amount of time you have available to grade it, and what you wish to measure. Some goals and methods of testing, adapted from Fuhrmann and Grasha (1983) are:

- To measure *knowledge* (recall of common terms, facts, principles, and procedures), ask students to define, describe, identify, list, outline, or select.
- To measure *application* (solving problems, applying concepts and principles to new situations), ask students to demonstrate, modify, prepare, solve, or use.
- To measure *analysis* (recognition of unstated assumptions or logical fallacies, ability to distinguish between facts and inferences), ask students to diagram, differentiate, infer, relate, compare, or select.
- To measure *comprehension* (understanding of facts and principles, interpretation of material), ask students to convert, distinguish, estimate, explain, generalize, define limits for, give examples, infer, predict, or summarize.
- To measure *synthesis* (integration of learning from different areas or solving problems by creative thinking), ask students to categorize, combine, devise, design, explain, or generate.
- To measure *evaluation* (judging and assessing), ask students to appraise, compare, conclude, discriminate, explain, justify, or interpret.

There are a limited number of standard formats for exam questions. Multiple choice questions can measure students' mastery of details, specific knowledge as well as complex concepts. Because multiple choice test items can be answered quickly, you can assess students' grasp of many topics in an hour exam. Although multiple choice test items are easily scored, good multiple choice questions can be challenging to write (see sidebar on page 42). Short answer questions can

Writing Effective Multiple Choice Questions

One of the best ways to identify useful wrong answers for multiple-choice items is first to ask the question in a free-response format. When the free-response tests are graded, look for common errors or misconceptions and tally them. If what went wrong is not clear from a students' response, ask the student to explain how he or she went about answering the question when the papers are returned. Then use common errors as the wrong answers for multiple-choice questions.

After several years of this activity—less if you share items with colleagues—you will have a sizable bank of good multiple choice questions and understand common misconceptions and errors well enough to construct suitable multiple-choice questions without going through the preliminary step of giving free-response items first.

Herron, 1996

require one or two sentences or brief paragraphs. They are easier to write than multiple choice tests but take longer to score, and may not be as useful as essay exams to measure the depth of student understanding. Essay questions probe students' understanding of broad issues and general concepts. They can measure how well students are able to organize, integrate, and synthesize material and apply information to new situations. Unlike multiple choice tests, you can only pose a few essay questions in an hour. Further, essay tests are sometimes difficult to grade.

Problem solving forms the core of many science courses, and numerical problems are prominent on many exams in these courses. As noted in Chapter 4, students who successfully answer these test questions do not necessarily grasp the underlying concept (Gabel and Bunce, 1994). Traditional numeric problems can incorporate some sort of conceptual essay section which measures the students' understanding of the concepts involved as well as their ability to use algorithms to solve problems. Nakhleh and Mitchell (1993) offer a sample of multiple choice questions for a limited number of chemistry concepts, in which the answers are pictorial representations of molecular events. Although you may find it difficult to develop an appropriate set of possible answers (see sidebar on multiple choice tests), asking students to draw a picture of the phenomenon described in the numerical problem is a good way to test their conceptual understanding.

Keep in mind that novice problem solvers take longer to locate appropriate strategies than experienced problem solvers. As a rule of thumb, it could take students ten minutes to solve a problem you might do in two minutes, so plan your test length accordingly. There are several resources to help faculty members develop, administer, and grade exams (Jacobs and Chase, 1992; Davis, 1993; Ory and Ryan, 1993).

What About Take-Home Tests?

With take-home tests, students generally work at their own pace with access to books and materials and the Internet. At institutions with a strong honor code, some faculty members provide strict guidelines about the time limit and the resources students can use on take-home tests. Take-home questions can be longer and more involved than in-class questions. Problem sets, short answer questions, and essays are the most appropriate for take-home exams. Some suggestions for giving take-home tests include:

- Limit the number of words that students write.
- Give students explicit instructions on what they can and cannot do, such as: Are they allowed to talk to other students about their answers? Can they work in groups? Be explicit about the consequences of violating these rules.

An alternative to a take-home test is to give out the questions in advance but ask the students to write their answers in class.

Are There Advantages to Open Book Tests?

Some instructors feel that open-book tests are inappropriate for introductory courses in which very basic concepts or facts are being learned. On an open-book test, students who lack basic knowledge may waste too much time consulting references and searching for information. Although open-book tests tend to reduce student anxiety, some research has shown that students do not necessarily perform significantly better on open-book tests, and that open-book tests seem to reduce students' motivation to study (Clift and Imrie, 1981; Crooks, 1988). A compromise between open- and closed-book testing is to include with the closed book test any appropriate reference material such as equations, formulas, constants, or unit conversions.

HELPING YOUR STUDENTS PREPARE FOR EXAMS

How can you help your students do better on exams? Distributing practice exams, scheduling extra office hours before a test, arranging for review sessions before major exams, and encouraging students to study in groups (particularly in which they share solution strategies, not just answers) are all excellent ways to allay students' anxieties and enhance their performance. Early success in a course may also increase students' motivation and confidence. It is a good idea to advise students carefully before the first exam, as it often sets the tone for the rest of the course. Here are some tips for helping students prepare for tests:

- Distribute sample questions and old exams to give an idea of the types of questions used.
- Review with students the thought processes involved in answering test questions.
- Review lists of questions and show students how to sort them by the type of reasoning or the type of solution required.
- Use quizzes and midterm exams to indicate the types of questions that will appear on the final exam.

TESTING STUDENTS THROUGHOUT THE TERM

Although many students dislike frequent tests, periodic testing during the term has been shown to improve students' performance on the final exam (Lowman, 1995). Giving two or more midterm exams also spreads out the pressure, allows students to concentrate on one chunk of material at a time, and permits students and instructors to monitor student progress more carefully. By giving students many opportunities to show what they know, faculty members can acquire a more accurate picture of students' abilities and avoid penalizing students who have an off day. For first- and second-year courses, it is common for an instructor to schedule two midterms; several shorter tests, quizzes, or writing assignments; and a final exam.

After a test, most students are anxious to see how they have done. It is a good idea to discuss the overall results in class. Returning work to students as quickly as possible encourages them to learn from their mistakes. One way to encourage this is to require students to resubmit a corrected

---

Tips to Students on How to Solve Exam Problems

- read the problem carefully and identify the information that is specifically requested
- list all "givens," both explicit and implicit
- break the problem into smaller parts
- do the easiest parts or steps first
- make a rough approximation of what the solution should look like

exam. The section below on ways to encourage improvement suggests a number of ways to reflect this effort in a student's course grade.

APPROACHES TO ASSIGNING GRADES

Many faculty members, especially new instructors, feel uneasy about assigning course grades. According to Erickson and Strommer (1991), how faculty members view grades depends a great deal on their values, assumptions, and educational philosophy. For example, some faculty members consider their introductory courses for science and engineering majors to be "weeder" classes designed to separate out students who lack potential for future success in the field and they assign grades accordingly. A problem with this philosophy is that students who are weeded out leave the course with a very poor perception of science and scientists. It is important to keep in mind that even in courses intended for students who will continue in the major, the majority of students are not planning to major in that field; physics courses taken by chemistry majors and chemistry courses taken by biology majors are but two examples. Courses for non-scientists generally fall into this category. Although most faculty members see grades as a measure of how well a student has mastered information, skills, and the ability to reason scientifically, some faculty members include other factors such as classroom participation, effort, or attendance.

There are two general approaches to assigning grades: criterion-referenced grading and norm-referenced grading. In *criterion-referenced grading*, students' grades are based on an absolute scale established by the instructor before the exam is graded. If all the students in a class achieve 80 percent or higher on an exam, they will all receive A's or B's. Conversely, if none of the students in a class scores better than 80 percent, then no one in the class receives a grade higher than B- for that test. Criterion-referenced grading meets three important standards: any number of students can earn A's and B's; the focus is on learning and mastery of material; final grades reflect what students know, compared to the teacher's standards. There are various ways to identify the criterion (standard) for each letter grade. Ory and Ryan (1993) describe a strategy that involves determining the number of items on a test that students need to answer correctly to achieve a C (typically those items written at the basic knowledge or comprehension levels), adding to that minimum the number of additional items for a B (questions written at higher levels) and for an A, and then working back to D and F. Criterion-referenced grading requires skill and experience in writing exams and establishing the grading scale. New teachers are advised to consult with experienced colleagues before using this approach.

Secondly, *norm-referenced grading*, often called grading on a curve, measures a student's achievement relative to other students in the class. Faculty members uncomfortable with setting absolute standards or unsure of the difficulty level of their exams may chose to grade on a curve as a way to renormalize the class scores. Many traditional grading systems used in science classes put students in competition with their classmates and limit the number of high grades. Research indicates that normative systems such as grading on the curve can reduce students' motivation to learn, and increase the likelihood

---

Helping Students Learn from Exams

Students often learn more from their tests if there are detailed written comments about their errors. Try commenting on individual tests or posting a key that includes a preferred solution method, alternative solutions, and commentary on common errors and the flaws in the reasoning behind them. Words of encouragement on students' papers mean a lot to them, and can motivate them to study harder for the next test or work harder on the next assignment.

What Do the Numbers Mean?

Science and mathematics teachers are quantitatively skilled, but how accurate, objective, and meaningful are their test scores? Despite the apparent objectivity of the numerical result, it is important to remember that there is subjectivity in the selecting and weighting of questions and in assigning numerical values or deducting points for missing parts of answers. The uncertainty of the numbers depends on how those scores were determined.

Scoring Your Tests

When scoring a test, as with designing, it is a good idea to decide whether the objective is to see what students know and what they have learned or to identify specific things they do not know or cannot do. The objectives of the test are implicit in its design and grading rubric. In any case, a specific scoring strategy (giving points for things done or deducting points for missing items) is recommended. If questions have multiple parts, plan your scoring strategy so that students who stumble on the first part do not lose all of the points. Many teachers find it easiest and most uniform to grade all students on a particular question at the same time. Keeping the student's identity unknown as you grade the test is also a good practice, because it helps minimize any bias in grading.

of academic dishonesty and evaluation anxiety (Crooks, 1988; McKeachie, 1994). Normative grading also serves to discourage effective group studying or other work, because assisting a classmate inherently decreases the value of the work of other students in the class. In addition, a grade assigned on the curve does not indicate how much or how little students have learned, only where they stand in relation to the class. Some faculty members try to compensate for inequities by adjusting the cutoff scores or by assigning a higher percentage of A's than usual if the class is especially good.

Another form of norm-referenced grading is to assign grades according to breaks in the distribution. In this model, scores are arranged from highest to lowest, and notable gaps or breaks in the distribution are located. For example, on a midterm totaling 100 points, eight students score 81 or higher and three students score 75; no one scores between 80 and 76. Instructors using this model will assign A's to students who scored 81 and above, and start the B's at 75. One disadvantage of this assumption is that these breaks may not represent true differences in achievement, so the magnitude of the gaps in scores should be taken into account. A further disadvantage of this model of grading is that the grade distribution depends on judgments made after students have taken the test rather than on guidelines that are established before testing.

When students' scores are fairly well distributed across a wide range, different approaches often yield similar grades. However, if the overall performance of the class is either low or high, the model used matters a great deal. When many students have done well on an exam, for example, everyone who did well will receive an A or B under criterion-referenced grading. When many students have done poorly, grading on a curve ensures that at least some will receive A's or B's.

Ways to Encourage Improvement

If you want to reward improvement, one way is to give students bonus points at the end of the term to acknowledge steady improvement throughout the semester. Alternatively, some instructors offer students a chance to drop a weak exam grade, replace it with their performance on a comprehensive final exam, or complete some credit-granting exercise which demonstrates an improved understanding of the material covered on the exam. Other faculty members allow students to correct their exams and resubmit their answers for a specified amount of additional credit.

7

Choosing and Using Instructional Resources

- What issues should I consider when selecting instructional materials?
- How can I use electronic resources to enhance student learning?
- How can I help my students use textbooks more effectively?

A key feature of effective teaching is the selection of instructional materials that meet the needs of students and fit the constraints of the teaching and learning environment. There are many pressures for educators to match the audiovisual stimuli of television, computers, and electronic games with which students are experienced. The speed of personal computers and the ease of authoring systems permit instructors to design and customize computer-based audiovisual presentations and to develop computer-based assignments for their students. The tremendous increases in rates of information transfer, access to the Internet, and posting of materials on the World Wide Web give instructors and students an almost limitless supply of resource material. In addition, the ease of electronic communications between an instructor and students, and among students, provides new opportunities for sharing questions, answers, and discussions during a course. At the same time, there remains a major role for student use of textbooks and for instructional use of demonstrations, films, videos, slides, and overhead transparencies.

Carefully scripted presentations and activities run the risk of emphasizing teacher delivery rather than student learning. Carefully planned and prepared instructional resources sometimes tempt instructors to race ahead and to cover more. The rapid-fire presentations combined with audiovisual overload can tempt students to remain intellectually passive. One way to avoid this is to intersperse activities which assess student understanding and encourage reflection and critical thinking. Another possibility is to reduce the pace of the class session, by pausing periodically to invite questions.

Instructional resources usually fall into one of two categories: student-centered and teacher-centered. In the student-centered model, instructional resources can be used for tutorials, problem solving, discovery, and review. In the teacher-centered model, resources are used for presentations of supplementary or primary material in the classroom as described in some examples in Chapter 2. Information technology can also be used for communication and for information retrieval.

TEXTBOOK USE IN TEACHING AND LEARNING

The mode of teaching so common today—the lecture-text-exam approach—is an artifact of centuries of European education. The professor's main role before the wide availability of the printing press was to lecture on information obtained from a rare copy of an often ancient book. Despite the fears of the faculty at the University of Salamanca during the sixteenth century, the textbook rapidly became a useful supplement to the class lecture rather than its replacement. Today a textbook is available for almost every college science class. As McKeachie (1994) notes, ". . . my years of experience in attempting to assess teaching effectiveness have led me to think that the textbook, more than any other element of the course, determines student learning."

Advantages and Disadvantages of Using Textbooks

Books are a highly portable form of information and can be accessed when, where, and at whatever rate and level of detail the reader desires. Research indicates that, for many people, visual processing (i.e., reading) is faster than auditory processing (i.e., listening to lectures), making textbooks a very effective resource (McKeachie, 1994). Reading can be done slowly, accompanied by extensive note taking, or it can be done rapidly, by skimming and skipping. There are advantages to both styles, and you may find it useful to discuss their merits with your students.

One important aspect of any science class is helping the student to make sense of the mass of information and ideas in a field. This can be done by showing students how to arrange information in a meaningful hierarchy of related major and minor concepts. Well-chosen textbooks help students understand how information and ideas can be organized.

Textbooks have several major limitations. Although a well-written book can engage and hold student interest, it is not inherently interactive. However, if students are encouraged to ask questions while they read, seek answers within the text, and identify other sources to explore ideas not contained in the text, they will become active readers and gain the maximum benefit from their textbook. In order to meet the needs of a broad audience, texts are often so thick that they overwhelm students seeking key information. Texts are often forced to rely on historical or dated examples, and they rarely give a sense of the discovery aspects and disorganization of information facing modern researchers.

Issues to Consider When Selecting Instructional Resources

- **What is the effect of the resources, methodologies, and technologies on student learning?**
- **How are students using them?**
- **What are students learning from them?**
- **Which students are using them?**
- **How and to what extent are students using optional resources?**

Changes in Textbook Style and Content

Science textbooks have evolved considerably from the descriptive and historical approaches common before World War II. Today's texts are far more sophisticated, less historical, and contain more facts than in the past, with complex language and terminology (Bailar, 1993). Illustrations and mathematical expressions are more common. Emphasis has shifted toward principles and theory. Modern texts attempt to deal with issues of process as well as matters of fact or content. They are replete with essays, sidebars, diagrams, illustrations, worked examples, and problems and questions at many different levels. One result of these changes is that the average book length has increased two to four times in the past several decades.

In response to the need for quality science textbooks for all students, not just science majors, some authors are returning to descriptive and historical approaches. Generally, books for science literacy courses describe important ideas and discoveries, present a limited number of fundamental concepts, and emphasize the links among different facts and principles. Others (e.g., Trefil and Hazen, 1995) take an interdisciplinary approach, by covering a range of science disciplines in a coherent, connected manner.

Textbooks and Effective Learning

Research on the effectiveness of textbooks has focused on two general areas: text structure and layout. The study of text structure has focused on how the reader builds cognitive representations from text. Recent work categorizes the structure of science text as either a proof-first or a principle-first organization (Dee-Lucas and Larkin, 1990). The proof-first organization develops a proof or argument that builds to a conclusion, usually in the form of a fundamental concept, principle, or law. In principle-first organization, a concept or principle is stated explicitly, then the evidence needed to support it is presented. The prevalence of the proof-first structure in contemporary textbooks may be due to the fact that most college science textbooks are written by scientists with little formal training in education. They present science the way it is practiced by experts. However, studies by Dee-Lucas and Larkin (1990) indicate that the principle-first structure is more effective for long-term retention and understanding by novice readers.

Layout and illustrations are important predictors of a text's effectiveness. One of the most effective types of illustration, especially for students with low verbal aptitude, is a simple multicolor line drawing (Dwyer, 1972; Holliday et al., 1977). Although more visually appealing, and more prevalent in the current textbook market, realistic drawings or photographs are less effective at enhancing student learning. The organization of information on a page also affects student learning (Wendt, 1979).

How to Choose and Use an Appropriate Textbook

Before selecting a text, it is important to know what books are currently on the market. Colleagues who teach the same or a similar course (in your department or at other institutions) are good sources of ideas and information. Your campus bookstore's textbook manager can provide the name and phone number for textbook sales representatives from many different companies. Science education publications (see Appendix B) carry advertisements from major publishers, and some feature a book review section or annual book buyer's guide. Professional society meetings also provide a chance to talk to publishers and see their new textbooks. Many companies will supply review copies to potential textbook adopters, in return for information about the course in which it might be used.

There are a number of factors to consider when selecting a textbook. To be of greatest value to students, the objectives of a textbook must be consistent with those of the course. Authors often try to meet particular objectives in their books, and these may differ among the choices. Skim the preface to see whether you share the author's approach to the subject. Consider how the table of contents aligns with your course syllabus and teaching philosophy:

- Is coverage of topics broad or specific?
- Are key principles stated precisely and clearly?
- Are the explanations and interpretations consistent with your teaching style?

In addition to content, evaluate the text structure and layout as discussed in the previous section.ʼ Textbooks vary greatly in their level of difficulty with respect to readability, depth of theoretical treatment of information, and complexity of end-of-chapter problems. Colleagues who have adopted the book can provide insight about these issues. They are also helpful for determining whether a textbook contains errors, which have been shown to have a large, negative effect on student learning (Iona, 1987).

The text itself is rarely the only resource available to the students and instructor. Many publishers have a separate study guide, often with chapter summaries and solutions to textbook problems. Upon adoption of a text, publishers often provide (or offer for sale at a reduced price) transparencies, slides, and computer test banks. Software to accompany textbooks is also becoming more popular. This software can vary considerably in quality and usefulness, so you may want to ask for a demonstration disk before purchasing it or requiring that students purchase it.

Once you have chosen a textbook, help your students use it effectively. A number of suggestions are given in the sidebar. Allow time during the first week of class to introduce the text and outline your strategy for its use. Encourage your students to use the text by asking them questions that require higher-order critical thinking skills drawing on and extending its material, methods, or examples. Simple factual questions are of little value to long-term retention or true understanding. Higher-order questions require students to think about the readings, ask questions, integrate material, and develop answers in their own words.

When appropriate, help students to understand that a textbook is not always the final authority on a topic, particularly in fields where new information is discovered at a very fast rate. Students may learn that it is okay to question the text if the instructor also openly disagrees with some interpretations or approaches in the book. The instructor can use different interpretations as examples of unresolved problems and illustrate critical thinking by presenting reasons and evidence for differing opinions. However, be careful not to develop such a negative attitude toward the text that students stop using it, or question the teacher's judgment for choosing it.

Considerations in Choosing a Textbook

- **Look at it from the point of view of novice users. Is it accessible? Is it clear? Is it organized in a useful way?**
- **Consider the information and the weight. A single large encyclopedic text, of which only certain chapters will be used, may be selected by a professor who thinks that students ought to have all of that text's material available. A book which is more appropriate for the course may be available, often at substantially lower cost to the student.**
- **Choose a book that contains most of the information that is needed, and supplement it with additional readings. This alerts students to the existence of other resources.**
- **Match the text to the audience in terms of its preparation and prior knowledge. The text should be readable from the students' point of view.**
- **Check the book carefully for errors.**

What If I Can't Find the "Perfect" Textbook?

After a thorough search, you may find that the book you want simply does not exist. Publishers have realized this and have taken steps to customize their products to meet faculty needs. It is possible to select certain chapters of a given book to be bound as a volume. It is also possible to

Suggestions to Students on How to Use a Textbook

- Study assigned readings before each class. Be prepared for questions, references to those readings, and other activities building on that material.
- Take notes in outline form as you read the text, indicate key points with a highlighter, note connections between sections, make lists of questions that come to mind or uncertainties, and pause frequently to summarize the key points of each section or chapter.
- Compare your lists of questions and your lists of key points with those of others in the class.
- Bring questions to class or recitation sections and ask the instructor to answer them.
- Review the text after the class to gain additional perspective.
- Look in supplemental texts to see how other authors present similar topics, especially if the points seem vague or unclear in the primary text. Remember that often the presentation that introduces new information, concepts, and vocabulary will seem foreign. Another presentation with a slightly different twist may help you see something differently or may confirm that you have identified key points.
- Review the text before exams and quizzes or periodically throughout the term.
- Study and review worked examples before attacking the homework problems. Read over questions, exercises, and problems that are not assigned and think about how to answer them. Group questions or problems by the topics they address or the methods required to solve them. Summarize by writing your own problems. Consult worked examples in other texts.

combine chapters of different books from the same publisher. This approach offers considerable flexibility, given that many smaller textbook publishers are now subsidiaries of larger corporations. Another option is to combine resources from several different publishers and to offer students a "coursepack" instead of a textbook. Many college bookstores and copy centers will work with faculty members to collect chapters, readings, and supplements. They obtain the required copyrights, and bind and sell custom-designed materials tailored for a particular course.

INFORMATION TECHNOLOGY USE IN TEACHING AND LEARNING

Internet

The Internet is an international high-speed electronic communications network (linking many local, regional, and national networks) which allows individuals at institutions or at home to access each other's computers for rapid communication or information retrieval. For some, the value of the Internet is that it allows users at remote locations to sign-on to computers where they have accounts, often using connection software called telnet. For others, rapid electronic communication and document sharing replaces phone conversations and meetings and facilitates collaboration.

Another major use of the Internet has been to provide free public access to documents in electronic form. Many individuals and organizations "post" documents on their own computers so that others can obtain electronic copies (without need for special accounts and passwords). File transfers can be made by FTP (file transfer protocol) software, and for many who have posted documents to their Web pages (see below), file transfers can be initiated by as little as the click of a button on the title of the document.

World Wide Web

The World Wide Web (WWW) is a system of linking information (text, sound, graphics, and video) in a way that allows for easy movement between related documents and sites. To use the Web you need a computer with special software that is called a browser, such as Lynx, Mosaic, Cello, or Netscape, or equivalent services available through commercial Internet providers. Highly detailed text, graphics, and videos are available on a wide array of topics.

The Internet and the ease of information viewing and retrieval that are possible through the Web mean that students are no longer limited to information provided by textbooks and printed materials in libraries. Students may "search" on the World Wide Web for preprints and reprints of articles, for discussion bulletin boards on specialized topics, for conference abstracts and proceedings, or for topical compilations of materials for research or teaching. Most Web navigational software systems include search engines that allow the user to locate information or sites by topic area. With more than a thousand new Web sites added every day, browsing for information on the Web needs to be done even more carefully than a literature search for library references. Bear in mind that while the Web holds enormous potential in providing access to information, much of the information available has not been reviewed for quality or reliability.

A number of electronic resources are available to those seeking information about education. Many professional societies have created Web pages with information about their educational initiatives and with links to other resources. Also, consider looking at the information posted by those who fund educational initiatives, including the National Science Foundation, the Howard Hughes Medical Institute, and the Department of Education. Other databases of references and curricular initiatives are provided by the NRC Committee on Undergraduate Science Education (http://www2.nas.edu/cusehome), Project Kaleidoscope (PKAL), the Eisenhower Clearinghouse, and the Educational Research Information Center (ERIC).

Examples of Faculty and Student Use of Web Resources

- **Course Web pages give students easy access to assigned readings and reference material.**
- **Student presentations to their classmates through creation of Web pages.**
- **Student access to resource information for papers or research projects.**
- **Access to discussion groups and the latest information on particular topics.**

Electronic Communication

Electronic mail ("e-mail") enables students and faculty to communicate with each other and with people all over the world. Many groups have adopted or created systems under which messages sent to a single address are delivered to mail accounts of all members of the group. This kind of electronic bulletin board is called a "listserv." A variation of a listserv bulletin board is a moderated listserv for which all messages are viewed by a moderator (and perhaps condensed, grouped, arranged, and/or edited) before being broadcast. Another form of group electronic communication is through a bulletin board on which messages are posted, called a newsgroup. Interested readers must sign on to a particular electronic address to find and read messages or posted documents. Bulletin boards of this type permit readers to leave their reactions to and comments on the postings of others.

Many instructors use electronic communication to facilitate interactions among students, and between students and themselves. Some faculty members create course-related Web pages with a mechanism for students to enter their comments or messages when they are connected to the Web page. Sample uses of e-mail or Web pages for communication include:

- Students send questions electronically to the instructor, which gives them an opportunity to express a doubt or misconception that they might have been afraid to voice in class. The instructor can transmit the question and the answer simultaneously to all students, without identifying the individual who asked the question.
- Students send or post questions about course material and are encouraged to answer each other's questions. Faculty members can monitor these exchanges to gauge student understanding and progress.
- Faculty hold "electronic office hours" in addition to traditional ones, so that students can ask a question and receive an answer almost immediately. This approach is becoming more common at institutions with a large commuter population, where students cannot always attend the faculty member's office hours.
- Faculty require drafts of student papers to be submitted electronically; not only does this make it easier for some faculty to review the draft, it forces the student to become familiar with technology used in the workplace.
- Faculty members distribute or post homework assignments, homework solutions, exam solutions, and other supplemental information electronically.
- Faculty create electronic "suggestion boxes" where students can post their comments about the course; consult the administrator of your campus e-mail system for ways to make the postings anonymous.

Choosing and Using Electronic Technologies

Before reviewing particular software, it is important to know which course goal it will help you to achieve. The next step is to talk to publishers, colleagues, and personnel from your campus's academic computing department. Lists such as those published by Boettcher (1993) and Kozma

---

Advantages of Interactive Computer Software

- **Increased motivation because software packages offer feedback and respond to the questions and uncertainties of the student.**
- **Increased enjoyment of learning because students shift from the passive role of receiving knowledge to the more active role of becoming seekers of knowledge.**
- **Reduced learning time due to personalized instruction which accommodates different learning styles.**
- **Self-paced instruction encourages the student to invest the time in weak areas rather than in areas they have already mastered.**
- **Increased retention from the enhanced engagement and participation of the learner.**
- **Mastery can be more nearly ensured because programs can be designed so that new material will not be covered until the current material is mastered by the student.**
- **Privacy because students interact on a one-on-one level and are free to ask questions without feeling intimidated or embarrassed.**
- **Opportunity to conduct simulated laboratory procedures and experiments which are too dangerous or expensive to be performed by students, or which require expensive laboratory equipment.**

and Johnson (1991) describe award-winning software developed by faculty members. Many software vendors offer demonstration disks that illustrate many of their products' features. In addition to working with the demonstration disks yourself, invite students to give you feedback on the product.

After purchasing software for student use, you should invest the time necessary to maximize its benefit to students. Some class time (or special sessions in a computer lab) may be needed to teach the students how to use the software effectively. If students will use the product outside of class, introduce the software to the staff at the campus computer labs, so that they will be prepared to answer students' questions. Faculty usually need to develop "courseware" to help guide the students through the software.

The great advantage of multimedia systems is that the combined audio and visual explanation helps students learn and remember. But to avoid student frustration with interactive systems, instructors should make their expectations clear and should provide opportunities for students to get assistance.

8

Getting to Know Your Students

- Knowing your students and helping them succeed
- Understanding students' biases, based on culture, gender, and societal differences
- Dealing with science fear and math anxiety
- Encouraging a positive attitude toward science

Each class brings a new group of students. Sometimes the course is new to the instructor as well. While teachers are responsible for course planning and scheduling of content, we should not forget the important effect our students' backgrounds have on learning (see discussions in Chapter 3). Getting to know students and getting to know about them are important prerequisites for effective teaching, especially since it is becoming increasingly likely that today's students will differ more in their demographics, preparations, attitudes, and interests than when we were undergraduates.

While students themselves are the most responsible for their own learning, good teachers should also accept responsibility for the learning of their students. Colleges and universities cannot focus solely on the delivery of content while assigning all responsibility for learning to the students. Teachers can do much to encourage and enhance learning both in classrooms and laboratories and outside of them. Teachers who continually try to understand their audiences and to address student interests, deficiencies, and misconceptions will be the most successful in helping students to meet their own responsibilities to learn.

Courses naturally differ in their intended audiences. Survey classes, for example, are intended to give a broad overview of a field, while other courses have a more narrow focus and are specifically designed for those who will take additional courses in a given discipline, whether or not they seek a career in that field. It is important for us to realize, however, that even in these specialized classes, many students will not complete the major. Moreover, every class is likely to have students who will themselves become teachers, and all science courses should be seen as an opportunity to influence the thinking and the scientific knowledge base of the citizenry.

Beliefs or preconceived notions about students influence how we teach. How we respond to our students, in turn, influences how they learn. What students believe about science and scientists affects what they hear, what they believe, how they study, and what they learn. Good teaching requires that we bridge the chasms of perception, language, background, and assumption that may impede effective communication and thereby hinder student learning.

Knowledge about students will enable the teacher to refine lectures, class discussions, comments, illustrations, and activities so that they are more effective learning experiences. References to student interests, backgrounds, knowledge, and even anxieties can make the class seem more personal and the material more accessible.

LEARNING YOUR STUDENTS' NAMES

Our special efforts to get to know students' names can enhance their self-esteem and promote class participation. Most of us are overwhelmed by a large number of new faces and new names. However, memory of names and faces often can be triggered by associating them with some activity or event, such as a discussion after class about an assignment or the outcome of an examination. One way to create such memory-jogging events for names and faces is to ask students to write a half-page self-description or to introduce themselves to the class with a statement of their interests or goals. In return, we should offer our own statements of interests, reasons for teaching the course, and goals and expectations. If your class enrolls fewer than 40 students, call roll for several class meetings at the beginning of the term to help you learn names. During the term, call students by name when you return homework or quizzes, and use names frequently in class. Ask students who are not called upon by name to identify themselves.

Office hours or problem-solving sessions offer opportunities to get to know your students. Clearly defined and observed office hours mean a great deal to some students. If you offer to communicate with students by e-mail or voice mail, it is a good idea to tell them when the mail is checked and how quickly they can expect a response.

HELPING YOUR STUDENTS SUCCEED

Teachers should state their expectations clearly. If a routine for success in the course is envisioned, share it with the students. Students who succeed are usually those who attend class regularly, ask questions, come to office hours and problem-solving sessions, study outside class both alone and in study groups, seek to understand methods and overarching principles or concepts rather than specific answers, teach or tutor others, and discuss concepts informally with their fellow students.

In light of the varied backgrounds and expectations of students in most classrooms, it is essential that you know how to refer students to academic and other resources they are likely to need. Tutoring may be needed and expected espe-

---

Tips for Learning Students' Names

- **Use photographs. Group three or four students in a single Polaroid shot. The act of posing for a picture breaks the ice, and you can have students write their name underneath their picture.**
- **Arrive for class as early as you can and use this time to sit and talk to the students that are waiting for you to begin.**
- **Use name cards. For seminar classes, place name cards in front of each student. For lab courses, post students' names above their workstations.**
- **Use a seating chart. Ask students to sit in the same general area for the first few weeks and block out on a piece of paper general locations within the room and write the names of students inside the appropriate blocks. During the first class meeting, ask students to write on index cards answers to some simple questions about their background, interests, and motivation. Collect the cards and use them as memory aids as roll is called or papers and quizzes are returned.**
- **Find out about their experiences in other science courses, with the particular subject matter in this course, and especially in prerequisite courses.**
- **Arrange for regular informal lunches with different small groups of students.**
- **Early in the course, write personalized comments on assignments returned; invite students to come by to discuss their progress.**
- **Require students to pick up their exams in person to discuss the outcome briefly.**

cially in introductory courses. It should be provided before difficulties become overwhelming. Accordingly, you can be most helpful by providing students with opportunities for obtaining feedback, comment, and evaluation (short papers, quizzes, lab reports, etc.) early in the term.

You also may have to help students revise their expectations of tutoring. Some students come to tutoring for clarification, some expect to be shown how to get the answers, while others come to be shown the answers. It is important to explain what tutoring and problem sessions can do; what topics, questions, and problems will be addressed; and what students should do before, during, and after such sessions. Scheduling tutoring sessions before or after assignments are due emphasizes the function of the sessions.

A stigma can be attached to seeking tutoring services because needs or other deficiencies in preparation are viewed as signs of innate inability. However, the students who do best are usually those who take advantage of every learning situation. Tutoring and problem-solving sessions should be portrayed positively. These sessions are frequently the best opportunities for students to get to know the teachers and to see how they think. Methods and answers are important, but personal contact can be crucial to a student's success.

Finally, some students demonstrate what Paulos (1988) describes as extreme intellectual lethargy. These students seem to be so lacking in mental discipline or motivation that nothing can get through to them. Faculty members have described this group as having an "I dare you" attitude, as being indifferent at best and hostile at worst. Sometimes this behavior masks fear or poor preparation. Sometimes it signals a short attention span. It also may indicate a more serious systemic problem such as attention deficit disorder. Faculty members may want to refer these students to college or community services designed to assist them. Catching and holding the interest of these students in class require patience, perseverance, and ingenuity:

Students Are More Likely to Succeed If They:

- **come to class**
- **sit toward the front of the room**
- **take notes**
- **form study groups to prepare for classes and exams**
- **make use of campus resources such as writing centers and tutoring services**
- **read assigned material and review notes before each class**
- **come to each class with one or two questions**
- **summarize each class with a few key concepts learned or questions that remain**

- Call on a specific student.
- Ask the student for a counter example, doubt, or criticism of your presentation or argument.
- Ask students to confer and to report on agreements and disagreements. Use this opportunity to call specifically on disaffected students.
- Ask the student to participate in a laboratory or classroom demonstration.
- To aid those with shorter attention spans, break class periods into segments with changes in presentation strategy, level of student activity, and switching of student roles among questioning, note taking, musing, discussing, challenging, and summarizing.
- Invite the student to come in for a conference to discuss how the course and the student's attitude might be improved.

SCIENCE FEAR AND MATH ANXIETY

A common notion in our society is that the ability to understand mathematics and the sciences is inborn. This belief influences how many parents and K-12 teachers have reacted to these subjects, and their attitudes often have conditioned the attitudes of students. It can be difficult to convince students who believe they have no aptitude for mathematics that they can understand even the simplest mathematical relationships. Their belief can serve as a self-fulfilling prophecy, resulting in mathematics avoidance. Tobias (1978) showed how mathematics avoidance in high school resulted in some young women's lack of preparation for college-level mathematics and science courses. Although men may have math anxiety, women are more likely to be affected (Sadker and Sadker, 1994).

To investigate students' attitudes toward science, some faculty give a brief questionnaire on the first day of class. Useful information for understanding students includes their perceptions of the process of science, of scientists themselves, and of the concepts and topics to be presented in the course. Students' perceptions can be surprising. The answers to questions such as those posed below can guide you throughout the entire semester.

- What is science?
- What is meant by scientific thinking?
- How is science done by scientists?
- How do scientists monitor the validity of their work?
- How has scientific thought or a scientific discovery helped society?
- How has scientific information had a negative effect on society?
- How do scientists help society safeguard against abuses of science or technology?

Having students respond periodically throughout the term to these questions can lead to more effective teaching. While lecturing or leading discussions, the teacher can refer to responses and perceptions of individual students (without revealing their names). This gives students the sense that your lectures contain more dialogue than monologue and piques students' interest because their questions or opinions have become reference points in the presentations.

However, it is important that you refer to student responses carefully, even if the student's identity is not divulged. Making disparaging or condescending comments about a student's work can result in that student's developing negative attitudes about the course, the instructor, and the student's own abilities.

OTHER CONSIDERATIONS

External pressures that students face vary from school to school, and it is important for you to understand any particular situations of students enrolled in your courses. For example, fewer than 50 percent of college students in the fall of 1991 were 21 years old or younger. The older they were, the more likely they were to attend college part time while working full time or to attend full time while working part time to finance their education. Students can arrive at class tired from a day at work or having to juggle their class schedules so they can work. Many have family responsibilities. Others have been out of the work force for some time, may be changing careers voluntarily, or may be changing careers as the result of layoffs. They may feel either ill at ease attending classes with students young enough to be their children or alienated by a college environment that has changed since their earlier student days (Shields, 1995). At the same time, older students are often more focused, with clearer goals and interests (Grosset, 1991). Their life experiences can enrich class or group discussions.

Nearly seven percent of first-year students in the fall of 1993 said that English was not their first language (Astin et al., 1993). That number is expected to increase. Students who can converse in English and read the language reasonably well can still have difficulty learning the specialized vocabularies of the sciences and understanding classroom presentations, particularly in large lectures.

Cultural influences can affect how students think about science: reasoning by analogy or by strict linear logic; memorizing specific correct responses or generalizing; problem solving by induction or by deduction; or needing to learn through hands-on apprenticeships to gain one aspect of a skill before moving on to the next step (Kolodny, 1991). Cultural prohibitions permeate some societies; for example, values that discourage assertiveness, outspokenness, and competitiveness in some cultures result in behavior that can be interpreted as being indifferent, having nothing to say, or being unable to act decisively (Hoy, 1993). We should not assume that outspokenness, assertiveness, or expressed career goals indicate mastery or interest in a subject, or vice versa. Studies on the reasons that students switch from a science major to the humanities or social sciences suggest that minority students are far more likely to be influenced by others (such as family members) to choose a science major than are Caucasian students (Seymour and Hewitt, 1994). In some cases, minority students' choice of major was based more on career goals than on intrinsic interest in the subject matter, due in part to the prestige of a certain career (e.g., medicine, engineering). Awareness of these factors can help faculty be more sensitive to the needs and motivations of all students in their classes. Efforts should be taken to encourage all students and to avoid rewarding or penalizing students for personal styles or cultural values that differ from those of the majority.

You should find out if your students are unfamiliar with specialized language. Many words that scientists view as common are completely unknown to students. Several times during a term, ask students to jot down every unfamiliar word used in class that day. The words that appear most often on student responses should be defined and explained at the beginning of the next class. By showing an effort to speak in terms that students can understand, as well as teaching the students this new language and its vocabulary, teachers can help students to view themselves as partners in the learning process. By making it a practice not only to define technical terms but to point out routinely how the different parts of the unfamiliar term contribute to its meaning, students will become familiar with prefixes, suffixes, and roots of technical terms, and they will be better able to discern the meanings of other words that contain these elements.

You can assist underprepared students, especially those at the introductory level, by being sensitive to their needs. Students often lack numerical perspective, have an exaggerated appreciation for meaningless coincidence, or have a credulous acceptance of pseudosciences (Paulos, 1988). By better understanding the nature and extent of some of these problems in a class, you can tailor discussions, readings, and problem sets to address these difficulties directly rather than ignoring, overlooking, or avoiding them.

ACCOMMODATING STUDENTS' DIFFERENCES

Students will differ in what they know, how they study, when they study, and how they learn. It is important that you not expect or look for particular student characteristics. Instead, all forms of excellence should be encouraged and nurtured. It is of particular importance to recognize differences in how students learn (discussed in Chapter 3) and differences in how they participate in class activities (discussed in Chapter 2). Tobias (1990) reported that many bright non-science majors are discouraged by the lack of a big-picture approach showing the relationships between different concepts. Fewer lecture-only presentations and more group activities can help students experience and understand the exchange of ideas that is essential to science.

Using Inclusive Language Patterns and Examples

- **Use terms of equal weight when referring to parallel groups (e.g., men and women rather than men and ladies).**
- **Use both "he" and "she" during lectures, discussions, and in writing, and encourage students to do the same.**
- **Recognize that your students may come from diverse socioeconomic backgrounds.**
- **Refrain from remarks that make assumptions about your students' experiences, such as "Now, when your parents were in college . . . "**
- **Avoid comments about students' social activities that are based on assumptions about students' lifestyles or behavior.**
- **Try to draw case studies, examples, photos, slides, and anecdotes from a variety of cultural and social contexts.**

Davis, 1993

Teachers can help create a positive learning environment for all students. Society encourages the beliefs that only few have scientific or mathematical minds and that women are less able than men to learn science or to enter scientific professions (Sonnert and Holton, 1996). Teachers must take care not to set in motion self-fulfilling prophecies based on unproved assumptions regarding students' ability to learn.

An emerging body of research indicates that male and female students exhibit different classroom behaviors and that they are treated differently in class by faculty members (Tannen, 1991; Sandler et al., 1996). Both women and men are prone to gender-biased teaching techniques involving interruptions of student responses, eye contact, modes of addressing students, and stereotypical examples or generalizations (Henes, 1994). Although most faculty members value class participation, male students are more likely to be vocal in class, and teacher behaviors often encourage this difference. Women appear more likely to discuss issues in small groups, especially single-gender groups, than in large classes. Teachers who work to become conscious of gender-related differences and to involve all students will be the most successful in encouraging the learning of both female and male students.

Regardless of a faculty member's background, the diversity of cultures in today's classrooms ensures that some students in each class will be from cultures that differ from the instructor's. Faculty members must not seek to clone themselves or to value unfairly their own traits that are mirrored in some students.

An important issue is whether special activities are needed to recruit and retain women and people of color in the sciences. According to Gibbons (1993), the most important factor in helping students of color to succeed in mathematics and science courses is the personal interest and backing of a faculty member. He suggests inviting students from underrepresented groups to join research labs; being sensitive to concerns of minority students; and being aware that they may need help in finding networks. Project Kaleidoscope's report to the National Science Foundation about what works in undergraduate science courses at liberal arts colleges indicates that cooperative activities, active learning, and connections with practicing researchers and research activities improve the learning environment for all students (Project Kaleidoscope, 1991)

Many students respond best to people with whom they can identify. For some, this means same-gender role models with similar cultural and ethnic backgrounds. Visitors to class and appropriate examples can help to diversify the role models presented in a class. However, white faculty members can serve as mentors to students from underrepresented groups, and male faculty members can serve as mentors to women students. Faculty members of color cannot be expected to meet all of the usual faculty responsibilities and, in addition, serve on all institutional human relations committees and mentor all of the students of color. Women faculty members should not have to shoulder the entire burden of mentoring women. Personal style may often be more important than demographic characteristics for successfully matching mentors to students.

Science teachers can help create positive attitudes toward science and mathematics by encouraging students to work together on research projects. Departments can establish discipline-specific study rooms, where students can find and interact with others in their courses. These can also serve as a meeting place for small study groups, or as a place where teaching assistants conduct "office hours" to assist students.

SOCIETAL ATTITUDES

Most students have heard and used such expressions as "nerd" or "science nerd," ridiculing good study habits and interest in or dedication to studying science. Among high school students, intelligence, intellectual curiosity, and excellence in mathematics and science can detract from popularity in some social circles.

A commonly held view is that understanding simple phenomena is possible for the average person but that understanding science is not. Some students are easily discouraged by their inability to grasp immediately the concepts presented in class. Teachers need to have the patience and the conviction to convince students that they can learn. How a teacher relates to students can either reinforce or provide counterexamples to stereotypical societal attitudes. For example, inappropriate stereotypes can be endorsed by faculty members by their choices of pronouns, their examples of scientists and nonscientists, how they select students to answer questions, what questions they ask of different students, and how they listen to or interrupt students who are asking or answering questions.

HELPING STUDENTS TO REALIZE THAT SCIENCE IS A HUMAN ENDEAVOR

Most students respond positively to activities such as visiting a professor's research lab, hearing about a professor's research, and viewing video clips of scientists explaining new discoveries. It can be very helpful to incorporate such activities into an introductory science class, despite the temptation to get on with the "real" science or the pressure to cover all of the content. One option is to begin each class with a brief discussion of an event in the day's newspaper or heard during a news broadcast that has a scientific component, so that students appreciate the connections between science and everyday experience. Many faculty members have found it fruitful to spend just a few minutes early in the semester sharing the results of their own work with the students in a way that explains the creation of ideas, development of proposals and receipt of funding, data collection and testing, paper writing and peer review, and presentation at meetings. Those teachers who serve on committees that advise government bodies or act in other public service roles can share stories of these efforts to show how science and society interact.

Appendix A

Societies and Organizations Involved with Science Teaching and Science-Related Issues

SCIENCE TEACHING SOCIETIES AND ORGANIZATIONS

American Association for Higher Education
One Dupont Circle, Suite 600
Washington, DC 20036-1110
(202) 293-6440

American Association of Physics Teachers
1 Physics Ellipse
College Park, MD 20740-3845
(301) 209-3300

American Council on Education
One Dupont Circle, Suite 800
Washington, DC 20036
(202) 939-9300

Association for the Education of Teachers in Science
The University of West Florida
11000 University Parkway
Pensacola, FL 32514
(904) 474-2860

Association of American Colleges and Universities
1818 R Street, NW
Washington, DC 20009
(202) 387-3760

Biological Sciences Curriculum Study
5415 Mark Dabling Blvd.
Colorado Springs, CO 80918-3482
(719) 531-5550

Carnegie Foundation for the Advancement of Teaching
1755 Massachusetts Avenue, NW
Washington, DC 20036
(202) 387-7200

Coalition for Education in the Life Sciences
Office of Education and Training
American Society for Microbiology
1325 Massachusetts Avenue, NW
Washington, DC 20005
(202) 737-3600

Council of Chief State School Officers
One Massachusetts Avenue, NW, Suite 700
Washington, DC 20001-1431
(202) 408-5505

Council of Graduate Schools
One Dupont Circle, Suite 430
Washington, DC 20036
(202) 223-3791

Independent Colleges Organization
1730 Rhode Island Avenue, NW
Washington, DC 20036
(202) 232-1300

National Association for Research in Science Teaching
Ohio State University
1929 Kenny Rd., Suite 100
Columbus, OH 43210-1015
(614) 292-3339

National Association of Biology Teachers
11250 Roger Bacon Drive, Suite 19
Reston, VA 22090
(703) 471-1134

National Association of Geoscience Teachers
c/o Robert A. Christman
P.O. Box 5443
Bellingham, WA 98227-5443
(360) 650-3587

National Center for Improving Science Education
2000 L Street, NW, Suite 603
Washington, DC 20036
(202) 467-0652

National Center on Postsecondary Teaching, Learning, and Assessment
The Pennsylvania State University
403 South Allen Street, Suite 104
University Park, PA 16801-5252
(814) 865-5917

National Council of Teachers of Mathematics
1906 Association Drive
Reston, VA 20191-1593
(703) 620-9840

National Earth Science Teachers Association
c/o M. Frank Watt Ireton
American Geophysical Union
2000 Florida Avenue, NW
Washington, DC 20009
(202) 462-6910x243; (202) 328-0566

National Science Teachers Association
1840 Wilson Blvd.
Arlington, VA 22201-3000
(703) 243-7100

Society for College Science Teachers
c/o Dr. William McIntosh
Delaware State University
Dover, DE 19901
(302) 739-5206

State Higher Education Executive Officers
707 17th Street, Suite 2700
Denver, CO 80202-3427
(303) 299-3600

SCIENCE AND TECHNOLOGY-RELATED ORGANIZATIONS

American Association for the Advancement of Science
1333 H Street, NW
Washington, DC 20005
(202) 326-6400

American Association of Medical Colleges
2450 N Street, NW
Washington, DC 20037
(202) 828-0400

American Astronomical Society
2000 Florida Avenue, NW
Suite 400
Washington, DC 20009
(202)328-2010

American Chemical Society
1155 16th Street, NW
Washington, DC 20036
(202) 872-4600

American Geological Institute
4220 King Street
Alexandria, VA 22302
(703) 379-2480

American Geophysical Union
2000 Florida Avenue, NW
Washington, DC 20009
(202) 462-6900

American Institute of Biological Sciences
1444 I Street, NW, Suite 2000
Washington, DC 20001-4521
(202) 628-1500

American Institute of Physics
1 Physics Ellipse
College Park, MD 20740-3843
(301) 209-3007

American Mathematical Association of Two-Year Colleges
State Technical Institute at Memphis
5983 Macon Cove
Memphis, TN 38134
(901) 383-4643

American Mathematical Society
1529 18th Street, NW
Washington, DC 20036
(202) 588-1100; (800) 321-4267

American Physical Society
1 Physics Ellipse
College Park, MD 20740-3843
(301) 209-3007

American Physiological Society
9650 Rockville Pike
Bethesda, MD 20814-3991
(301) 530-7118

American Society for Cell Biology
9650 Rockville Pike
Bethesda, MD 20814-3992
(301) 530-7153

American Society for Engineering Education
1818 N Street, NW, Suite 600
Washington, DC 20036
(202) 331-3500

American Society for Microbiology
1325 Massachusetts Avenue, NW
Washington, DC 20005
(202) 737-3600

Carnegie Commission on Science, Technology and Government
437 Madison Avenue
New York, NY 10022
(212) 371-3200

Geological Society of America
P.O. Box 9140
300 Penrose Place
Boulder, CO 80301
(303) 447-2020

Harvard-Smithsonian Center for Astrophysics
60 Garden Street
Cambridge, MA 02138
(617) 496-4798

International Center for the Advancement of Scientific Literacy
Chicago Academy of Sciences
2060 North Clark Street
Chicago, IL 60614
(312) 549-0606

Mathematical Association of America
1529 18th Street, NW
Washington, DC 20036
(202) 387-5200

Optical Society of America
2010 Massachusetts Avenue
Washington, DC 20036
(202) 223-8130

Science, Technology, and Society Program
133 Willard Building
University Park, PA 16802
(814) 865-9951

Sigma Xi, The Scientific Research Society
P.O. 13975
Research Triangle Park, NC 27611-7448
(919) 549-4691

ORGANIZATIONS FOR WOMEN IN SCIENCE, MATHEMATICS, AND ENGINEERING

American Association of University Women
1111 16th Street, NW
Washington, DC, 20036-4873
(202) 785-7700

Association for Women in Mathematics
4114 Computer and Space Science Building
University of Maryland
College Park, MD 20742-2461
(301) 405-7892

Association for Women in Science
1522 K Street, NW, Suite 820
Washington, DC 20005
(202) 408-0742

Society of Women Engineers
120 Wall Street
New York, NY 10005
(212) 509-9577

Appendix B

Periodicals Related to Undergraduate Science Education

GENERAL INTEREST

Journal of College Science Teaching
National Science Teachers Association
1840 Wilson Blvd.
Arlington, VA 22201-3000
(703) 243-7100

DISCIPLINARY JOURNALS

Biology

American Biology Teacher
National Association of Biology Teachers
11250 Roger Bacon Drive, Suite 19
Reston, VA 22090
(703) 471-1134

Journal of Biological Education
Institute of Biology
20-22 Queensberry Place
London, England SW7 202
0171-581-8333

Chemistry

Journal of Chemical Education
American Chemical Society
1155 16th Street, NW
Washington, DC 20036
(202) 872-4600

Engineering

Chemical Engineering Education
c/o Carole Yocum
Department of Chemical Engineering
University of Florida
Gainesville, FL 32611
(352) 392-0861

Prism
American Society for Engineering Education
1818 N Street, NW, Suite 600
Washington, DC 20036
(202) 331-3500

Geology/Earth Sciences

Journal of Environmental Education
Heldref Publications
1319 18th Street, NW
Washington, DC 20036-1802
(202) 296-6267

Journal of Geoscience Education (formerly the Journal of Geological Education)
National Association of Geoscience Teachers
c/o Robert A. Christman
P.O. Box 5443
Bellingham, WA 98227-5443
(360) 650-3587

Mathematics

College Mathematics Journal
Mathematical Association of America
1529 18th Street, NW
Washington, DC 20036
(202) 387-5200

Mathematics and Computer Education
MATYC Journal, Inc.
Box 158
Old Bethpage, NY 11804
(516) 822-5475

Mathematics Teacher
National Council of Teachers of Mathematics
1906 Association Drive
Reston, VA 22091
(703) 620-9840

Physics

American Journal of Physics
American Association of Physics Teachers
1 Physics Ellipse
College Park, MD 20740-3845
(301) 209-3300

Physics Education
Institute of Physics, London
IOP Publishing, Ltd.
Techno House
Redcliffe Way
Bristol, England
Avon BS1 6NX
0117-929-7481

The Physics Teacher
American Association of Physics Teachers
1 Physics Ellipse
College Park, MD 20740-3845
(301) 209-3300

Women in Science

Journal of Women and Minorities in Science & Engineering
Women's Research Institute
Virginia Polytechnic Institute & State University
10 Sandy Hall
Blacksburg, VA 24061-0338

SCIENCE EDUCATION RESEARCH JOURNALS

International Journal of Science Education
Taylor & Francis Ltd.
Rankine Road
Basingstoke, Hants RG24 8PR
England
01256-840366

Journal of Research in Mathematics Education
National Council of Teachers of Mathematics
1906 Association Drive
Reston, VA 22091
(703) 620-9840

Journal of Research in Science Teaching
National Association for Research in Science Teaching
John Wiley & Sons, Inc.
605 Third Avenue
New York, NY 10158
(212) 850-6645

Journal of Science Teacher Education
National Association for Research in Science Teaching
Ohio State University
1929 Kenny Rd., Suite 100
Columbus, OH 43210-1015
(614) 292-3339

Research in Science Education
Center for Mathematics and Science Education
Queensland University of Technology
Locked Bag #2, Red Hill
Brisbane, Australia

Research in Science and Technological Education
Carfax Publishing Co.
P.O. Box 25
Abingdon, Oxon, OX14 3UE
England
01235 555-335

PSYCHOLOGY JOURNALS WITH ARTICLES RELEVANT TO SCIENCE EDUCATION

Child Development
Society for Research in Child Development
University of Chicago Press, Journals Division
5720 South Woodlawn Avenue
Chicago, IL 60637
(312) 753-0811

Cognition and Instruction
Lawrence Erlbaum Associates, Inc.
10 Industrial Drive
Mahwah, NJ 07430-2262
(201) 236-9500

Developmental Psychology
Journal of Educational Psychology
American Psychological Association
750 First Street, NE
Washington, DC 20002-4242
(202) 336-5600

Appendix C

Laboratory Issues

RESOURCES ON INQUIRY-BASED LABS

Attracting Students to Science: Undergraduate and Precollege Programs, Howard Hughes Medical Institute, Bethesda, Md., 1992.

Describes HHMI-funded projects, including laboratory projects, at 96 different colleges and universities.

BioQUEST Curriculum Consortium
John R. Jungck and Patti Soderberg, Directors
Department of Biology, Beloit College
700 College Street
Beloit, WI 53511
(608) 363-2743
bioquest@beloit.edu

The BioQUEST Curriculum Consortium is a consortium of biologists, science education researchers, historians and philosophers of biology, computer scientists, academic computing specialists, designers, cognitive psychologists, curriculum theorists, and others who are committed to transforming biology education through the extensive use of research and research-like experiences in learning biology. Members are interested in issues related to teaching and learning biology, the use of technological innovations, and the potential impact of these technologies on learning theory and the structure of schools. One of BioQUEST's major goals is the creation and dissemination of innovative and flexible instructional learning tools and the establishment of a communication network for like-minded biology faculty.

Workshop Physics Project
Priscilla W. Laws
Department of Physics and Astronomy
Dickinson College
Carlisle, PA 17013
(717) 243-1242

The Workshop Physics project at Dickinson College represents an attempt to redesign the teaching methods in introductory physics courses to take advantage of recent findings in physics education research and introduce students to the use of modern computer tools. Students meet in three two-hour sessions each week. There are no formal lectures. The course content has been reduced by about 25 percent as compared with the normal curriculum. Each section has one instructor, two undergraduate teaching assistants, and up to twenty-four students. Each pair of students shares the use of a microcomputer and an extensive collection of scientific apparatus and other gadgets. Among other things, students pitch baseballs, whack bowling balls with rubber hammers, pull objects up inclined planes, attempt pirouettes, build electronic circuits, explore electrical unknowns, ignite paper with compressed gas, and devise engine cycles using rubber bands. The Workshop labs are staffed during evening and weekend hours with undergraduate teaching assistants.

Successful Approaches to Teaching Introductory Science Courses, William J. McIntosh and Mario W. Caprio, editors, Society for College Science Teachers, 1992.

This monograph contains descriptions of eleven unique introductory science courses. These courses are taught at a wide variety of institutions, from community colleges to research universities, and cover all of the sciences. Each paper contains an in-depth discussion of a particular course as well as some theoretical background about why the course was changed and designed. Some of the techniques described in the papers include having students design their own lab experiments, using computers to link lectures and laboratories, and requiring students to complete individual research projects.

RESOURCES ON UNDERGRADUATE RESEARCH ACTIVITIES

In addition to the organizations listed below, many professional societies (Appendix A) have committees or programs on undergraduate research in their field, and we urge you to contact them for specific information.

Council on Undergraduate Research
John G. Stevens, National Executive Officer
University of North Carolina at Asheville
One University Heights
Asheville, NC 28804-3299
cur@UNCA.edu

CUR's goal is to promote research in the sciences and mathematics at predominately undergraduate institutions. CUR publishes directories of departments whose faculty and students are involved in undergraduate research, holds regional and national conferences, publishes a newsletter, and has a National Information Center for Undergraduate Research at its national office in Asheville, N.C.

National Conferences on Undergraduate Research
c/o Professor Tom Werner
Union College
Department of Chemistry
Schenectady, NY 12308
wernert@gar.union.edu
(518) 388-6789 (fax)

National meetings are held every spring for undergraduate students in all fields to present the results of their research or artistic or scholarly work in oral and poster sessions. Over 1,200 students from all academic disciplines gather each year for these presentations by their peers from hundreds of colleges and universities.

LABORATORY SAFETY

Berry, K. O. 1989. Safety in the chemical laboratory: safety concerns at the local laboratory. J. Chem. Educ. 66(2):A58-A60.

Furr, A. K., ed. 1990. CRC Handbook of Laboratory Safety, 3rd ed. Boca Raton, Fla.: CRC Press.

Gannaway, S. P. 1990. Chemical handling and waste disposal issues at liberal arts colleges. J. Chem. Educ. 67(7):A183-84.

Gass, J. R. 1990. Chemistry, courtrooms, and common sense. Part I: Negligence and duty. J. Chem. Educ. 67(1):51-55.

Mahn, W. J. 1991. Fundamentals of Laboratory Safety: Physical Hazards in the Academic Laboratory. New York: Van Nostrand Reinhold.

National Research Council, Committee on Prudent Practices for Handling, Storage, and Disposal of Chemicals in Laboratories. 1995. Prudent Practices in the Laboratory: Handling and Disposal of Chemicals. Washington, D.C.: National Academy Press.

Rayburn, S. R. 1990. The Foundations of Laboratory Safety: a Guide for the Biomedical Laboratory. New York: Springer-Verlag.

References

American Association for the Advancement of Science. 1990a. The Liberal Art of Science. Washington, D.C.: American Association for the Advancement of Science.

American Association for the Advancement of Science. 1990b. Science for All Americans. New York: Oxford University Press.

American Association for the Advancement of Science. 1993. Benchmarks for Science Literacy. New York: Oxford University Press.

American Psychological Association. 1992. Learner-Centered Psychological Principles: Guidelines for School Redesign and Reform. Washington, D.C.: American Psychological Association.

Anderson, C., and K. Roth. 1992. Teaching for meaningful and self-regulated learning of science. In Advances in Research on Teaching, Vol. 1., J. Brophy, ed. Greenwich, Conn.: JAI.

Angelo, T. A., and K. P. Cross. 1993. Classroom Assessment Techniques: a Handbook for College Teachers, 2nd ed. San Francisco: Jossey-Bass.

Arons, A. B. 1983. Achieving wider scientific literacy. Daedalus Spring:91-122.

Arons, A. B. 1990. A Guide to Introductory Physics Teaching. New York: John Wiley and Sons.

Astin, A. W., W. S. Korn, and E. R. Riggs. 1993. The American Freshman: National Norms for Fall 1993. Los Angeles: Higher Education Research Institute, UCLA.

Bailar, J. C. 1993. First-year college chemistry textbooks. J. Chem. Educ. 70:695-698.

Basili, P. A., and P. J. Sanford. 1991. Conceptual change strategies and cooperative group work in chemistry. J. Res. Sci. Teaching 28(4):293-304.

Baxter-Hastings, N. 1995. Workshop Mathematics: Gateway Courses, access via WWW: http://aug3.augsburg.edu/pkal/aboutpkal.html

Benson, D. L., M. C. Wittrock, and M. E. Baur. 1993. Students' preconceptions on the nature of gases. J. Res. Sci. Teaching 30:587-597.

Berry, D. A. 1987. A Potpourri of Physics Teaching Ideas. College Park, Md.: American Association of Physics Teachers.

Birk, J. P., and J. Foster. 1993. The importance of lecture in general chemistry course performance. J. Chem. Educ. 70:180-182.

Blackburn, T. 1995. From email discussion list posted to cur-l@listserv.ncsu.edu on Feb. 15, 1995, subject Scientific misunderstandings, by David Houseman. The archive for this list is located at listserv@ncsu.edu.

Boettcher, J. V., ed. 1993. 101 Success Stories of Information Technology in Higher Education. New York: McGraw-Hill.

Bonwell, C. C., and J. A. Eison. 1991. Active Learning: Creating Excitement in the Classroom. ASHE-ERIC Higher Education Report No. 1. Washington, D.C.: The George Washington University, School of Education and Human Development.

Braskamp, L., and J. Ory. 1994. Assessing Faculty Work: Enhancing Individual and Institutional Performance. San Francisco: Jossey-Bass.

Brooks, J. G., and M. G. Brooks. 1993. The Case for Constructivist Classrooms. Alexandria, Va.: Association for Supervision and Curriculum Development.

Brown, D., and J. Clement. 1991. Classroom teaching experiments in mechanics. In Research in Physics Learning: Theoretical Issues and Empirical Studies, R. Duit, F. Goldberg, and H. Niedderer, eds. San Diego, Calif.: San Diego State University.

Caprio, M. W. 1993. Cooperative learning: the crown jewel among motivational-teaching techniques. J. Coll. Sci. Teaching 22:279-281.

Cashin, W. E. 1990. Student ratings of teaching: recommendations for use. Idea Paper No. 22. Manhattan, Kans.: Center for Faculty Evaluation and Development in Higher Education, Kansas State University.

Cheek, D. W. 1992. Thinking Constructively about Science, Technology, and Society Education. Albany, NY: SUNY Press.

Chickering, A. W., and Z. F. Gamson. 1987. Seven principles for good practice in undergraduate education. Washington, D.C.: American Association of Higher Education. AAHE Bulletin, March:3-7

Claxton, C. S., and P. H. Murrell. 1987. Learning Styles: Implications for Improving Educational Practices. ASHE-ERIC Higher Education Report No. 4. Washington, D.C.: Association for the Study of Higher Education.

Clement, J., D. E. Brown, and A. Zietsman. 1989. Not all preconceptions are misconceptions: finding 'anchoring conceptions' for grounding instruction on students' intuitions. Int. J. Sci. Educ. 11:554-565.

Clift, J. C., and B. W. Imrie. 1981. Assessing Students, Appraising Teaching. New York: John Wiley and Sons.

Cooper, M. M. 1995. Cooperative learning: an approach for large enrollment courses. J. Chem. Educ. 72:162-164.

Craik, F. M., and R. S. Lockhart, 1972. Levels of processing: a framework for memory research. J. Verbal Learning Verbal Behav. 11:671-684.

Crooks, T. J. 1988. The impact of classroom evaluation practices on students. Rev. Educ. Res. 58(4):438-481.

Davis, B. G. 1993. Tools for Teaching. San Francisco: Jossey-Bass.

Dee-Lucas, D., and J. H. Larkin. 1990. Organization and comprehensibility in scientific proofs, or "Consider a Particle p. . . ." J. Educ. Psychol. 82:701-714.

Dressel, P. L., and D. Marcus. 1982. On Teaching and Learning in College. San Francisco: Jossey-Bass.

Dwyer, F. M. 1972. The effect of overt responses in improving visually programmed science instruction. J. Res. Sci. Teaching 9:47-55.

Ebel, R. L., and D. A. Frisbie. 1986. Essentials of Educational Measurement, 4th ed. Englewood Cliffs, N.J.: Prentice-Hall.

Eble, K. E. 1988. The Craft of Teaching. San Francisco: Jossey-Bass.

Edgerton, R., P. Hutchings, and K. Quinlan. 1991. The Teaching Portfolio: Capturing the Scholarship in Teaching. Washington, D.C.: American Association of Higher Education.

Erickson, B. L., and D. W. Strommer. 1991. Teaching College Freshmen. San Francisco: Jossey-Bass.

Esiobu, G. O., and K. Soyibo. 1995. Effects of concept and vee mapping under three learning modes on students' cognitive achievement in ecology and genetics. J. Res. Sci. Teaching 32:971-995.

Fraher, R. 1984. Suggestions for beginning teachers. Pp. 116-127 in The Art and Craft of Teaching, M. M. Gullette, ed. Cambridge, Mass.: Harvard University.

Fraser, B. J., and K. Tobin. 1989. Student perceptions of psychosocial environment in classrooms of exemplary science teachers. Int. J. Sci. Educ. 11:19-34.

Fraser, B. J. 1986. Classroom Environment. London: Croom Helm.

Freier, G. D., and F. J. Anderson. 1981. A Demonstration Handbook for Physics (2nd ed.). College Park, Md.: American Association of Physics Teachers.

Fuhrmann, B. S., and A. F. Grasha. 1983. A Practical Handbook for College Teachers. Boston: Little, Brown.

Gabel, D. L., and D. M. Bunce. 1994. Research on problem solving: chemistry. Pp. 301-326 in Handbook of Research on Science Teaching and Learning, D. L. Gabel, ed. New York: MacMillan.

Gardner, H. (1993). Multiple Intelligences: The Theory into Practice. New York: Basic Books.

Gibbons, A. 1993. White men can mentor: help from the majority. Science 262:1130-1134.

Glynn, S. W., and R. Duit. 1995. Constructing Conceptual Models. Pp. 1-33 in Learning Science in the Schools: Research Reforming Practice, S. W. Glynn and R. Duit, eds. Mahwah, N.J.: Lawrence Erbaum Associates.

Goodsell, A. S., M. R. Maher, V. Tinto, B. L. Smith, and J. MacGregor. 1992. Collaborative Learning: A Sourcebook for Higher Education. University Park, Pa.: National Center on Postsecondary Teaching, Learning, and Assessment.

Grosset, J. M. 1991. Patterns of integration, commitment and student characteristics and retention among younger and older students. Res. Higher Educ. 32(2):159-178.

Hake, R. R. 1992. Socratic pedagogy in the introductory physics lab. Physics Teacher 30:546.

Henes, R. 1994. Creating Gender Equity in Your Teaching. Davis, Calif.: College of Engineering, University of California, Davis.

Herron, J. D. 1996. The Chemistry Classroom: Formulas for Successful Teaching. Washington, D.C.: American Chemical Society.

Hinton, H. 1993. Reliability and validity of student evaluations: Testing models versus survey research models. PS: Political Science and Politics September: 562-569.

Holliday, W. G., L. L. Brunner, and E. L. Donais. 1977. Differential cognitive and affective responses to flow diagrams in science. J. Res. Sci. Teaching 14:129-138.

Hoy, R. R. 1993. A 'model minority' speaks out on cultural shyness. Science 262:1117-1118.

Hutchings, P. 1996. Making Teaching Community Property: A Menu for Peer Collaboration and Peer Review. Washington, D.C.: American Association for Higher Education.

Iona, M. 1987. Why Johnny can't learn physics from textbooks I have known. Am. J. Physics 55:299-307.

Jacobs, L. C., and C. I. Chase. 1992. Developing and Using Tests Effectively: A Guide for Faculty. San Francisco: Jossey-Bass.

Johnson, D. W., and R. T. Johnson. 1989. Cooperation and Competition: Theory and Research. Edina, Minn.: Interaction Book Co.

Johnson, D. W., R. T. Johnson, and K. A. Smith. 1991. Active Learning: Cooperation in the College Chemistry Classroom. Edina, Minn.: Interaction Book Co.

Joshi, B. D. 1991. Electronic reports and grading templates for multiple section freshman chemistry laboratories. J. Comput. Math. Sci. Teaching 10(3):37-49.

Kandel, M. 1989. Grading to motivate desired student performance in a descriptive laboratory course. J. Col. Sci. Teaching 18(4):249-251.

Katz, D. A. 1991. Science demonstrations, experiments, and resources: a reference list for elementary through college teachers emphasizing chemistry with some physics and life science. J. Chem. Educ. 68(3):235-244.

Koballa, T. R. 1995. Children's attitudes toward learning science. Pp. 59-84 in Learning Science in the Schools: Research Reforming Practice, S. W. Glynn and R. Duit, eds. Mahwah, N.J.: Lawrence Erbaum Associates.

Kolodny, A. 1991. Colleges must recognize students' cognitive styles and cultural backgrounds. Chronicle Higher Educ. 37(21):A44.

Kozma, R. B., and J. Johnson. 1991. The technological revolution comes to the classroom. Change 23(1):10-23.

Lambert, L. M., and S. L. Tice. 1993. Preparing Graduate Students to Teach. Washington, D.C.: American Association for Higher Education.

Laws, P. 1991. Calculus based physics without lectures. Physics Today Dec:24-31.

Lehman, J. D., C. O. Carter, and J. B. Kahle. 1985. Concept mapping, vee mapping, and achievement: results of a field study with black high school students. J. Res. Science Teaching 22:663-673.

Lisensky, G., L. Parmentier, and B. Spencer. 1994. Introductory chemistry at Beloit College. Leadership: Challenges for the Future (Occasional paper II). Washington, D.C.: Project Kaleidoscope.

Lowman, J. 1995. Mastering the Technique of Teaching. Second edition. San Francisco: Jossey-Bass.

Marsh, H. W., and M. J. Dunkin. 1992. Students' evaluation of university teaching: a multi-dimensional perspective. In Higher Education: A Handbook of Theory and Research, Vol. 8. New York: Agathon Press.

Mayer, M. 1987. Common sense knowledge versus scientific knowledge: the case of pressure, weight and gravity. Pp. 299-310 in Proceedings of the Second International Seminar: Misconceptions and Educational Strategies in Science and mathematics, Vol. 1. Ithaca, N.Y.: Cornell University Press.

Mazur, E. 1996. Conceptests. Englewood Cliffs, N.J.: Prentice-Hall.

McDermott, L. C. 1990. A perspective on teacher preparation in physics and other sciences: the need for special science courses for teachers. Am. J Phys. 58(8):734-742.

McDermott, L. C. 1991. What we teach and what is learned—closing the gap. Am. J. Physics 59:301-315.

McDermott, L. C., M. Rosenquist, and E. Van Zee. 1987. Student difficulties in connecting graphs and physics: examples from kinematics. Am. J. Physics 55:503-513.

McDermott, L.C., P. Shaffer, and M. Somers. 1994. Research as a guide for curriculum development: an illustration in the context of the Atwood's machine. Am. J. Phys. 62:46-55.

McDermott, L.C., and P. Shaffer. 1992. Research as a guide for curriculum development: an example from introductory electricity. Part I: Investigation of student understanding. Am. J. Phys. 60:994-1003.

McKeachie, W. J. 1994. Teaching Tips: Strategies, Research, and Theory for College and University Teachers, 9th ed. Lexington, Mass.: D. C. Heath and Company.

Meyers, C., and T. B. Jones. 1993. Promoting Active Learning: Strategies for the College Classroom. San Francisco: Jossey-Bass.

Minstrell, J. 1989. Teaching science for understanding. Pp. 129-149 in Toward the Thinking Curriculum: Current Cognitive Research, L. Resnick and L. Klopfer, eds. Alexandria, Va.: Association for Supervision and Curriculum Development.

Moog, R., and J. Farrell, 1996. Chemistry: A Guided Inquiry. New York: John Wiley and Sons.

Moore, J. A. 1984. Science as a way of knowing: evolutionary biology. Am Zoologist 24:421-534.

Murray, H. G. 1991. Effective teaching behaviors in the college classroom. Pp. 135-172 in Higher Education: Handbook of Theory and Research, Vol. 7. J. C. Smart, ed. New York: Agathon.

Nakhleh, M. B., and R. C. Mitchell. 1993. Concept learning versus problem solving: There is a difference. J. Chem. Educ. 70(3):190-192.

National Center for Improving Science Education. 1991. The High Stakes of High School Science. Washington, D.C.: National Center for Improving Science Education.

National Research Council. 1996. National Science Education Standards. Washington, D.C.: National Academy Press.

National Science Teachers Association. 1992. The Content Core, Vol. I. Arlington, Va.: National Science Teachers Association.

Novak, J. D. 1977. A Theory of Education. Ithaca, N.Y.: Cornell University.

Novak, J. D., and D. B. Gowin. 1984. Learning How to Learn. New York: Cambridge University Press.

O'Brien, T. 1991. The Science and Art of Science Demonstrations. J. Chem Ed. 68:933-936.

Okebukola, P. A., and O. J. Jegede. 1988. Cognitive preference and learning mode as determinants of meaningful learning through concept mapping. Sci. Educ. 74:489-500.

Ory, J. C., and K. E. Ryan. 1993. Tips for Improving Testing and Grading. Newbury Park, Calif.: Sage.

Orzechowski, R. F. 1995. Factors to consider before introducing active learning into a large, lecture-based course. J. Coll. Sci. Teaching 24(5):347-349.

Paulos, J. A. 1988. Innumeracy: Mathematical Illiteracy and Its Consequences. New York: Hill and Wang.

Pearsall, M. K., ed. 1992. Scope, Sequence, and Coordination. Vol. II, Relevant Research. Washington, D.C.: National Science Teachers Association.

Pintrich, P. R. 1988. Student learning and college teaching. Pp. 61-86 in College Teaching and Learning: Preparing for New Commitments. New

Directions for Teaching and Learning, No. 33. R. E. Young and K. E. Eble, eds. San Francisco: Jossey-Bass.

Posner, H. B., and J. A. Markstein. 1994. Cooperative learning in introductory cell and molecular biology. J. Coll. Sci. Teaching 23:231-233.

Posner, G., K. Strike, P. Hewson, and W. Gertzog. 1982. Accommodation of a scientific conception: toward a theory of conceptual change. Sci. Educ. 66(2):211-227.

A Private Universe. 1989. Cambridge, Mass.: Harvard-Smithsonian Center for Astrophysics.

Project Kaleidoscope. 1991. What Works: Building Natural Science Communities. Washington, D.C.: Project Kaleidoscope.

Reynolds, A. 1992. What is competent beginning teaching? A review of the literature. Rev. Educ. Res. 62:1-35.

Rondini, J. A., and J. A. Feighan. 1978. An ongoing grading technique for laboratory courses. J. Chem. Educ. 55(3):182-183.

Rowe, M. B. 1974. Wait time and rewards as instructional variables, their influence in language, logic, and fate control: Part 1. Wait time. J. Res. Sci. Teaching 11(2):81-94.

Sadker, M., and D. Sadker. 1994. Failing at Fairness: How America's Schools Cheat Girls. New York: Macmillan Publishing Company.

Sandler, B., L. Silverberg, and R. Hall. 1996. The Chilly Classroom Climate: a Guide to Improve the Education of Women. Washington, D.C.: The National Association for Women in Education.

Seymour, E., and N. M. Hewitt. 1994. Talking About Leaving. Factors Contributing to High Attrition Rates Among Science, Mathematics, and Engineering Undergraduate Majors: Final Report to the Alfred P. Sloan Foundation on an Ethnographic Inquiry at Seven Institutions. Boulder, Colo.: University of Colorado.

Shakhashiri, B. Z. 1983. Chemical Demonstrations: A Handbook for Teachers of Chemistry, Volume 1. Madison: University of Wisconsin Press.

Shakhashiri, B. Z. 1985. Chemical Demonstrations: A Handbook for Teachers of Chemistry, Volume 2. Madison: University of Wisconsin Press.

Shakhashiri, B. Z. 1989. Chemical Demonstrations: A Handbook for Teachers of Chemistry, Volume 3. Madison: University of Wisconsin Press.

Shakhashiri, B. Z. 1992. Chemical Demonstrations: A Handbook for Teachers of Chemistry, Volume 4. Madison: University of Wisconsin Press.

Shields, N. 1995. The link between student identity, attributions, and self-esteem among adult, returning students. Sociological Perspectives 38(2):261-272.

Shuell, T. J. 1990. Cognitive conceptions of learning. Rev. Educ. Res. 60(4):531-547.

Shulman, L. 1990. Aristotle had it right: on knowledge and pedagogy (Occasional paper no. 4). East Lansing, Mich.: The Holmes Group.

Silberman, M. 1996. Active Learning. Boston: Allyn and Bacon.

Slavin, R., 1989. Research on cooperative learning: consensus and controversy. Educ. Leadership, 47(4):52-54.

Smith, M. E., C. C. Hinckley, and G. L. Volk. 1991. Cooperative learning in the undergraduate laboratory. J. Chem. Educ. 68:413-415.

Sonnert, G., and G. Holton. 1996. Career Patterns of Women and Men in the Sciences. Am. Sci. 84:63-71.

Stepans, J. 1994. Targeting Students' Misconceptions: Physical Science Activities Using the Conceptual Change Model. Riverview, Fla.: Idea Factory, Inc.

Stover, S. T., G. A. Neubert, and J. C. Lawlor. 1993. Creating interactive environments in the secondary school. Washington, D.C.: National Education Association.

Summerlin, L. R., and J. L. Ealy, Jr. 1985. Chemical Demonstrations: A Sourcebook for Teachers. Washington, D.C.: American Chemical Society.

Summerlin, L. R., C. L. Bogford, and J. B. Ealy. 1987. Chemical Demonstrations: A Sourcebook for Teachers, Volume 2. Washington, D.C.: American Chemical Society.

Tannen, D. 1991. Teachers' classroom strategies should recognize that men and women use language differently. Chron. Higher Educ. 37(40): B1-B4.

Theall, M., and J. Franklin, eds. 1990. Student ratings of instruction: issues for improving practice. New Directions for Teaching and Learning, No. 43. San Francisco: Jossey-Bass.

Thornton, R. K. In press. Microcomputer-based labs and interactive lecture demonstrations. In Proceedings of the Conference on the Introductory Physics Course, J. Wilson, ed. New York: John Wiley and Sons.

Tobias, S. 1978. Overcoming Math Anxiety. New York: W. W. Norton & Company.

Tobias, S. 1990. They're Not Dumb, They're Different: Stalking the Second Tier. Tucson, Ariz.: Research Corporation.

Tobias, S. 1992. Revitalizing Undergraduate Science: Why Some Things Work and Most Don't. Tucson, Ariz.: Research Corporation.

Tobin, K., D. J. Tippins, and A. Gallard. 1994. Research on instructional strategies for teaching science. Pp. 45-93 in Handbook of Research on Science Teaching and Learning, D. L. Gabel, ed. New York: MacMillan.

Trefil, J., and R. M. Hazen. 1995. The Sciences: An Integrated Approach. New York: John Wiley and Sons.

Treisman, U., and R. E. Fullilove. 1990. Mathematics achievement among African American undergraduates at the University of California, Berkeley: an evaluation of the mathematics workshop program. J. Negro Educ. 59:463-478.

Urbach, F. 1992. Developing a teaching portfolio. Coll. Teaching 41(2):71-74.

Watson, S. B., and J. E. Marshall. 1995. Effects of cooperative incentives and heterogeneous arrangement on achievement and interaction of cooperative learning groups in a college life science course. J. Res. Sci. Teaching 32:219-299.

Wendt, D. 1979. An experimental approach to the improvement of the typographic design of textbooks. Visible Language 13:108-133.

West, I., and A. Pines. 1985. Cognitive Structure and Conceptual Change. New York: Academic Press.

Whimbey, A. 1986. Problem Solving and Cognition. Mahwah, N.J.: Lawrence Erlbaum Associates.

Wilson, J. M. 1994. The CUPLE physics studio. The Physics Teacher. 32:518-523.

Winograd, P., and G. Newell. 1984. Strategic difficulties in summarizing texts. Reading Res. Quarterly 19(4):404-425.

Witkin, H. A., and D. R. Goodenough. 1981. Cognitive Styles: Essence and Origins. New York: International Universities Press.

Woods, D. R. 1995. Teaching and learning: what can research tell us? J. Coll. Sci. Teaching. 25:229-232.

Index

(*Page numbers in italics refer to text in sidebars.*)

E

E-mail, 52-53, 56
Education of future teachers
  conceptual approaches, 7
  importance of, 7

G

Gender differences, 58, 60-61
Genetics, *13*
Geology, *11*
Goals
  as component in syllabus
    planning, 5-6
  for discussion sessions, 15
  for laboratory work, 16-17
  for nonscience majors, 3-4
  student diversity, 3
  student testing, 41
  student's understanding of
    science as multi-disciplinary,
    7
  for teaching, 9
Gould, James L., *17*
Grading
  bonus points, 45
  criterion-referenced systems, 44
  on a curve, 44
  of homework assignments, 39,
    40-41
  inherent subjectivity in, *45*
  norm-referenced systems, 44-45
  teacher attitudes, 39, 44
  test goals and, 39, *45*
  See also Assessment and
    evaluation of students;
    Testing
Grant, Rosemary, *6*
Group work
  collaborative learning, 15-16
  context for exploration, 24
  disadvantages, 16
  discussion sessions, 14-15
  grading, 40

H

Handouts, laboratory work, 18
Harvard University, *22*
Homework
  grading, 40-41
  take-home tests, 42

I

Information overload
  problems of discipline-centered
    approach, 4
  in instructional resources, 47
Information technology
  educational resources, 47, 51-54
  interactive software, *53*
  Internet, 51
  in laboratory work, 18
  software selection, 53
  teaching resources, 52
  World Wide Web, 52
Inquiry, 23
Inquiry-based labs, 73-74
Interdisciplinary courses, *5, 6,* 7
Internet, 51
Introductory courses, 4
  alternatives/enhancements to
    lecturing, 10-11
  grading policy, 44

J

Jones, Maitland, *6*

L

Laboratory work
  computer use, 18
  context for exploration, 24
  cooperative learning in, *18*
  grading, 39-40
  handling student questions, 12-
    13
  improving effectiveness of, 16-
    19
  inquiry-based, resources for, 73-
    74
  planning considerations, 18-19
  resources for planning, 17-18
  safety, publications on, 75
  significance of, for science, 16
  student reports, 19, *25*
  teaching assistants in, 19-20
  teaching goals, 16-17
  teaching technique, 18
  use of handouts, 18
Large classes
  alternatives to lecturing, 10-11
  demonstration projects for, 14
  discussion sections, 14
Learning
  allowing time for reflection, 24

best methods for, 4
  collaborative/cooperative, 15-16
  current conceptualization, 21-22
  from exams, *44*
  fundamental misconceptions as
    obstacles to, 27, 28-29
  overcoming misconceptions, 24
  process conceptualizations,
    research on, 26
  relationship with teaching, 2
  responsibility for, 55
  student evaluations of teachers
    and, 38
  student-teacher relations and,
    55-56
  styles of, 22-23
  teacher's goals for students, 3
  traditional conceptualizations of,
    21
  See also Active learning
Lecturing
  active learning in, 5
  alternatives, 10-11
  with discussion sections, 14
  handling student questions, 12-
    13
  limitations of, 9
  opportunities for improving, 11-
    12
  use of demonstration projects,
    13-14
Long, Sharon, *10, 13*

M

Mazur, Eric, *22*
Mentoring, 60-61
Minority students, 59, 60-61
Misconceptions
  as challenges to learning, 27,
    28-29
  examples, *29, 30*
  helping students confront, 29-30
  helping students overcome, 30-
    31
  identifying, 29
  as impediment to learning, 24
  resources for dealing with, 32
  science fear and math anxiety,
    57-58
  teaching strategies for dealing
    with, 29
  types of, 27-28
Molecular biology, *13*
Multimedia presentations, *11*

(Page numbers in italics refer to text in sidebars.)

(*Page numbers in italics refer to text in sidebars.*)